Communications in Computer and Information Science   493

Xiaodong Shi   Yidong Chen (Eds.)

Machine Translation

10th China Workshop, CWMT 2014
Macau, China, November 4-6, 2014
Proceedings

 Springer

Volume Editors

Xiaodong Shi
Xiamen University, Fujian, China
E-mail: mandel@xmu.edu.cn

Yidong Chen
Xiamen University, Fujian, China
E-mail: ydchen@xmu.edu.cn

ISSN 1865-0929   e-ISSN 1865-0937
ISBN 978-3-662-45700-9   e-ISBN 978-3-662-45701-6
DOI 10.1007/978-3-662-45701-6
Springer Heidelberg New York Dordrecht London

Library of Congress Control Number: 2014955083

Typesetting: Camera-ready by author, data conversion by Scientific Publishing Services, Chennai, India

Printed on acid-free paper

Springer is part of Springer Science+Business Media (www.springer.com)

Preface

The 10th China Workshop on Machine Translation (CWMT), which was held during November 4–6, 2014, in Macau, aimed to bring together researchers and practitioners in the field of machine translation (MT) and provide a forum to facilitate communication and exchange among domestic and foreign scholars on the latest developments in the field of MT, with a special emphasis on the languages in China.

Following the success of the first CWMT in Xiamen in 2005, nine successful workshops were organized, including five Machine Translation evaluations (2007, 2008, 2009, 2011, 2013), an open source systems' development (2006), and two strategic meetings (2010, 2012). These activities have made a substantial impact on fostering the research and development of MT technologies in China. CWMT is currently considered as a leading and important academic event in the natural language processing field in China.

The first Machine Translation Evaluation and Workshop was held successfully in Xiamen University, jointly organized by: the Institute of Automation, Chinese Academy of Sciences; Institute of Computing Technology, Chinese Academy of Sciences; and Xiamen University. Subsequent workshops were jointly organized by the Institute of Computing Technology, Chinese Academy of Sciences; Institute of Automation, Chinese Academy of Sciences; Institute of Software, Chinese Academy of Sciences; Harbin Institute of Technology; and Xiamen University. CWMT was organized successfully in different places between 2006 and 2013, including: Xiamen University; the Institute of Computing Technology, Chinese Academy of Sciences; Harbin Institute of Technology; Institute of Automation, Chinese Academy of Sciences; Nanjing University; Institute of Software, Chinese Academy of Sciences; Xi'an University of Technology; and Kunming University of Science and Technology. This year, CWMT 2014 was organized by Macau University.

CWMT 2014 featured keynote speeches delivered by renowned experts in the field of MT; panel discussions and tutorials exploring leading-edge technologies and applications in MT; and a best student paper award given during the conference. An exhibition of commercial and research systems was held during the conference bringing together the users, developers, and researchers of MT. This conference offered them a great opportunity to share and exchange valuable experiences in MT, and thus to advance MT research and development in the region.

This year's paper submission was made through the EasyChair conference system. We received a total of 29 papers, among which 27 were from China. All the papers are carefully reviewed in a double-blind manner and each paper was assigned to three independent reviewers.

It was the first time that CWMT used EasyChair for the review phase. The review process is divided into four steps:

1. After the submission deadline has passed, all the reviewers are notified so that they can bid for the papers they like to review most (5 days). Most of the reviewers are Program Committee members of the previous CWMT workshops.
2. The reviewing process begins (15 days). Every paper is assigned to three reviewers. If a paper is not chosen by any reviewer, it is assigned randomly by EasyChair.
3. The first round of the review process ends, and the author response period (5 days) begins.
4. The reviews may change the accept/reject decision according to the author response. And in some cases, the Program Committee chair is involved. After 7 days, authors are then notified about the status of their papers.

Finally, 11 Chinese and 11 English papers were accepted (one accepted English paper was withdrawn at the end). The accepted papers address all aspects of MT, including preprocessing, language modeling, MT models, MT evaluation, and application to the patent translation, with a focus on MT of Chinese from/to minority languages. We believe that the publication and presentations of all these papers will advance the state of the art of MT research in China and on Chinese.

Last but not least, this is the first time that the conference proceedings (English manuscripts) of CWMT are published by Springer in the *Communications in Computer and Information Science* series, which we hope will draw more attention to this conference.

October 2014   Xiaodong Shi

Organization

Honorary Chair

Philip C.L. Chen   University of Macau

Conference Chair

Tiejun Zhao   Harbin Institute of Technology

Program Chair

Xiaodong Shi   Xiamen University

Tutorial Chair

Qun Liu   Institute of Computing Technology, Chinese Academy of Sciences (CAS-ICT)

Panel Discussion Chair

Jinbo Zhu   Northeastern University

Publication Chair

Yidong Chen   Xiamen University

Program Committee (sorted according to Pinyin)

Dongfeng Cai	Shenyang Institute of Aeronautical Engineering
Cai Rangjia	Qinghai Normal University
Hailong Cao	Harbin Institute of Technology
Wenhan Chao	Beihang University
Boxing Chen	ICT-NRC, Canada
Jiajun Chen	Nanjing University
Yidong Chen	Xiamen University
Jinhua Du	Xi'an University of Technology
Xiangyu Duan	Suzhou University
Guohong Fu	Heilongjiang University
Yanqing He	Institute of Scientific and Technical Information of China
Zhongjun He	Baidu

Degen Huang	Dalian University of Technology
Yeyan Huang	Beijing Institute of Technology
Hongfei Jiang	National Patent Information Center
Wenbin Jiang	Institute of Computing Technology, Chinese Academy of Sciences (CAS-ICT)
Mu Li	Microsoft Research Asia
Qun Liu	Institute of Computing Technology, Chinese Academy of Sciences (CAS-ICT)
Yang Liu	Tsinghua University
Yanjun Ma	Baidu
Yao Meng	Fujitsu Research & Development Center
Na Shunwuritu	Mongolia University
Xiaodong Shi	Xiamen University
Le Sun	Institute of Software, Chinese Academy of Sciences (CAS-IS)
Türgün Ibrahim	Xinjiang University
Haifeng Wang	Baidu
Hua Wu	Baidu
Fei Xia	University of Washington
Tong Xiao	Northeastern University
Deyi Xiong	Suzhou University
Jinan Xu	Beijing Jiaotong University
Endong Xun	Beijing Language and Culture University
Muyun Yang	Harbin Institute of Technology
Yusup Abaydul	Xinjiang Normal University
Zhengtao Yu	Kunming University
Jiajun Zhang	Institute of Automation, Chinese Academy of Sciences (CAS-IA)
Min Zhang	Soochow University
Yujie Zhang	Beijing Jiaotong University
Hongmei Zhao	Institute of Computing Technology, Chinese Academy of Sciences (CAS-ICT)
Tiejun Zhao	Harbin Institute of Technology
Yu Zhou	Institute of Automation, Chinese Academy of Sciences (CAS-IA)
Jingbo Zhu	Northeastern University
Chengqing Zong	Institute of Automation, Chinese Academy of Sciences

Local Organization Chairs

Derek F. Wong	University of Macau
Lidia S. Chao	University of Macau

Local Organizing Committee

Francisco Oliveira   University of Macau
Hoklam Sio   University of Macau
Wenghong Lam   University of Macau
Xiaodong Zeng   University of Macau
Liang Tian   University of Macau
Longye Wang   University of Macau

Organizers

Chinese Information Processing Society of China

Co-organizers

University of Macau

Faculty of Science and Technology, University of Macau

Sponsors

Fundo para o Desenvolvimento das Ciências e da Tecnologia

Table of Contents

Making Language Model as Small as Possible in Statistical Machine
Translation.. 1
    Yang Liu, Jiajun Zhang, Jie Hao, and Dakun Zhang

Data Selection via Semi-supervised Recursive Autoencoders for SMT
Domain Adaptation 13
    Yi Lu, Derek F. Wong, Lidia S. Chao, and Longyue Wang

Effective Hypotheses Re-ranking Model in Statistical Machine
Translation.. 24
    Yiming Wang, Longyue Wang, Derek F. Wong, and Lidia S. Chao

Recognizing and Reordering the Translation Units in a Long NP for
Chinese-English Patent Machine Translation 33
    Xiaodie Liu, Yun Zhu, and Yaohong Jin

A Statistical Method for Translating Chinese into Under-resourced
Minority Languages 49
    Lei Chen, Miao Li, Jian Zhang, Zede Zhu, and Zhenxin Yang

Character Tagging-Based Word Segmentation for Uyghur 61
    Yating Yang, Chenggang Mi, Bo Ma, Rui Dong, Lei Wang,
    and Xiao Li

Analysis of the Chinese - Portuguese Machine Translation of Chinese
Localizers *Qian* and *Hou* 70
    Chunhui Lu, Ana Leal, Paulo Quaresma, and Márcia Schmaltz

Chunk-Based Dependency-to-String Model with Japanese
Case Frame 80
    Jinan Xu, Peihao Wu, Jun Xie, and Yujie Zhang

A Novel Hybrid Approach to Arabic Named Entity Recognition........ 93
    Mohamed A. Meselhi, Hitham M. Abo Bakr, Ibrahim Ziedan,
    and Khaled Shaalan

Reexaminatin on Voting for Crowd Sourcing MT Evaluation 104
    Yiming Wang and Muyun Yang

Author Index 117

Making Language Model as Small as Possible in Statistical Machine Translation

Yang Liu[1], Jiajun Zhang[1], Jie Hao[2], and Dakun Zhang[2]

[1] NLPR, Institute of Automation, Chinese Academy of Sciences, Beijing, China
[2] Toshiba (China) R&D Center, Beijing, China
{yang.liu2013,jjzhang}@nlpr.ia.ac.cn
{haojie,zhangdakun}@toshiba.com.cn

Abstract. As one of the key components, n-gram language model is most frequently used in statistical machine translation. Typically, higher order of the language model leads to better translation performance. However, higher order of the n-gram language model requires much more monolingual training data to avoid data sparseness. Furthermore, the model size increases exponentially when the n-gram order becomes higher and higher. In this paper, we investigate the language model pruning techniques that aim at making the model size as small as possible while keeping the translation quality. According to our investigation, we further propose to replace the higher order n-grams with a low-order cluster-based language model. The extensive experiments show that our method is very effective.

Keywords: language model pruning, frequent n-gram clustering, statistical machine translation.

1 Introduction

In statistical machine translation (SMT), language model is one of the key components (others include translation model and reordering model). Typically, SMT applies a word-based n-gram language model which predicts the nth word using the previous n-1 words as the context. Although the n-gram language model ignores the intrinsic structure of the natural language, it is employed in almost all of the SMT models due to its simplicity and effectiveness.

Furthermore, it is well acknowledged that the higher the n-gram order (not too high), the better the SMT performance is. However, in order to avoid the data sparseness problem, higher n-gram language model needs much more training data for parameter estimation. Moreover, the size of the model increases exponentially with the order grows. In practical use, we usually require the language model size to be as small as possible while keeping its capacity as much as possible. Accordingly, many language model pruning techniques are proposed, including count-cutoffs (Jelinek et al., 1990), weighted difference pruning (and its variants) (Seymore and Rosenfeld, 1996; Moore and Quirk, 2009), Stolcke pruning (Stolcke, 1998), and IBM clustering (Brown et al, 1990). The previous works show that these pruning approaches perform

X. Shi and Y. Chen (Eds.): CWMT 2014, CCIS 493, pp. 1–12, 2014.

similarly with respect to the language model perplexity. But, few studies investigate the relationship between the pruning techniques (language model size) and the SMT performance.

In this paper, we aim at conducting a comprehensive investigation to figure out how the SMT performance is influenced by the language model pruning technique. For simplicity and efficiency, we just adopt the count-cutoff pruning technique with modified Knerser-Ney discounting. In this study, we investigate various pruning options and evaluate how they influence the translation quality of different SMT models (the conventional phrases-based model and the formal syntax-based model).

According to the deep analysis of the investigation results, we find an interesting phenomenon: many 4-gram and 5-gram instances share the same frequent trigram. Based on this finding, we propose a simple but effective approach that makes full use of the frequent trigrams and their contexts to replace all the 4-gram and 5-gram instances. We further propose to cluster the frequent trigrams with Brown Clustering and re-train a cluster-based trigram language model. By doing so, we hope the original trigram language model plus the new cluster-based trigram one can obtain the similar translation performance while retaining a small model size.

The extensive large-scale experiments demonstrate that the pruning technique can discard about half of the ngrams for the 5-gram language model while keeping the same translation performance as the original 5-gram language model. By clustering the frequent trigrams and retraining a new cluster-based trigram language model, we can keep the language model size as small as the original trigram language model, but can improve the translation quality over the original trigram one statistical significantly, although it still underperforms the 5-gram language model.

2   Language Model Pruning for Machine Translation

2.1   Language Model Pruning

In classical language modeling, the language model pruning aims to reduce the language model size as much as possible, as long as the language model perplexity does not increase. Conventionally, there are four well-known pruning techniques including count-cutoffs (Jelinek et al., 1990), weighted difference pruning (and its variants) (Seymore and Rosenfeld, 1996; Moore and Quirk, 2009), Stolcke pruning (Stolcke, 1998), and IBM clustering (Brown et al, 1990). As the n-gram model is widely adopted, the model pruning techniques usually attempt to remove the n-gram entries as many as possible.

For example, in the count-cutoffs pruning technique (Jelinek et al., 1990), any n-gram with the occurrence times below the pre-defined cutoff threshold will be discarded. This method can result in significantly small models, with slight increase in perplexity.

The weighted difference method (Seymore and Rosenfeld, 1996) focuses on the difference between the previous words. Considering the phrase "the Great Wall", if the bigram probability $P(Wall|Great)$ is the same as the trigram probability $P(Wall|the$ $Great)$, the trigram probability $P(Wall|the$ $Great)$ is unnecessary and the trigram entry "the Great Wall" will be discarded.

Stolck pruning (Stolcke, 1998) is a pruning approach which is based on relative entropy. Stolcke first calculate the relative entropy as follows:

$$\sum_{x,y,z} p(xyz)[log P'(z|xy) - log P(z|xy)] \tag{1}$$

Here, P' denotes the model after pruning, and P denotes the original model. Trigram probability $P(z|xy)$ will increase the entropy of the model. If the entropy increased by the particular trigram less than the pruning threshold, this trigram will be removed. It is shown that this method has similar result with the weighted difference method in practice.

IBM clustering (or Brown clustering) (Brown et al., 1990) is a word-based clustering technique. The idea of IBM clustering is that similar words always appear in similar context. Thus, the cluster of those words, called word class, can be used as a variable to substitute the original word and estimate the corresponding probability.

Goodman and Gao (2000) has conducted a comprehensive comparison for these four techniques in the purely language modeling. The results imply that although count-cutoff method is not the best choice in some cases, the difference on reduced size and perplexity between those pruning become negligible with increasing training data. Moreover, in Moore and Quirk's (2009) work, it is shown that the simple count cutoff method with modified Kneser-Ney discounting smoothing technique can achieve similar result with weighted-difference variant method.

From the pruning techniques in purely language modeling, count cutoff is a simple but effective approach. As few researchers study the relationship between the language model size and the translation quality, we choose the count cutoff technique with modified Kneser-Ney discounting smoothing to prune the language model in the machine translation scenario.

2.2   Language Model Pruning for The Phrase-Based Translation

In practical applications, the phrase-based model is the most popular model to construct the translation system due to its simplicity, effectiveness and efficiency. The phrase-based translation model generates the output from left to right by expanding one phrase translation each time. As one of the most key components, the language model attempts to distinguish the fluent translations from the ungrammatical outputs.

To prune the language model with the count cutoff technique, the only parameter is the count cutoff threshold. As mentioned in the previous section, any n-gram whose occurrence is below this threshold will be discarded. It should be noted that the count cutoff based n-gram pruning does not only affect the n-gram itself, but also influence the low order n-grams during the language model training.

We conduct our experiments on Chinese-to-English translation, using the state-of-the-art phrase-based system Moses (Koehn et al., 2007).We perform word alignment with GIZA++ (Och, 2000). The word alignments are symmetrized using the grow-diag-final-and heuristic. The bilingual training corpus comes from LDC[1], including

---

[1] LDC category numbers: LDC2000T50, LDC2002L27, LDC2003E07, LDC2003E14, LDC2004T07, LDC2005T06, LDC2005T10 and LDC2005T34.

about 2.1 million parallel sentence pairs. We apply the SRILM toolkit[2] (SRI Language Modeling Toolkit) to train the baseline n-gram language model with the modified Knerser-Ney discount smoothing using the target side of the bilingual training data plus the Xinhua portion of the English Gigaword corpus. To prune the baseline language model, we adopt the option "-gt*n*min" in the SRILM toolkit to investigate the relations between the language model size and the translation performance.

We use the NIST MT2003 test data as the development set, and NIST MT2004 as the test set. The evaluation metric is case-insensitive BLEU-4 with shortest length penalty.

Table 1 shows the statistics of the language model size and the translation quality using the baseline language model with n-gram order from 1 to 7. Each n-gram model is trained using the same modified Knerser-Ney discount smoothing technique.

Table 1. Performance of the phrase-based translation with each n-gram language model

Language Model	Size(MB)	BLEU	Perplexity
Unigram	32	22.31	1155.74
Bigram	458	29.76	201.90
Trigram	1,063	33.91	121.54
4-gram	2,036	35.37	107.64
5-gram	3,079	35.70	104.69
6-gram	4,046	35.72	103.95
7-gram	4,938	35.74	103.54

From Table 1, we can see that the improvement of the translation quality is very obvious when unigram is upgraded to bigram and trigram. However, the 6-gram or 7-gram models perform similar to the 5-gram model, but increase the model size a lot. Considering the balance between the model size and the translation performance, we choose the 5-gram model as our baseline. Our main task is to prune the 5-gram language model as much as possible.

To have a thorough investigation, we set the count cutoff threshold from 2 to 70, and see how the relation between the model size and translation quality changes. Figure 1 illustrates the statistics.

Figure 1 demonstrates that the language model size is reduced significantly with the threshold grows, but the translation quality does not decrease significantly ($p \leq 0.5$). In practice, we also test the performance with much stricter threshold (e.g. 100 ~ 500). It turns out that the translation performance drops significantly with the threshold around 100 while the language model size is almost unchanged.

2.3   Language Model Pruning for the BTG-based Translation

The BTG (Bracketing Transduction Grammars) based translation (Wu, 1997; Xiong et al., 2006; Zhang and Zong, 2009) can be viewed as a monolingual parsing process,

---

[2] SRILM is available at http://www.speech.sri.com/projects/srilm/

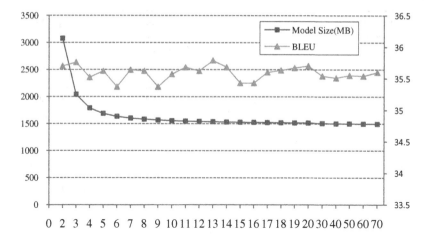

Fig. 1. Performance of the Phrase-based translation with pruned language model. The X-axis represents the threshold for pruning, and the Y-axis denotes the size of the pruned language model size and the translation quality (in BLEU scores).

· in which only lexical rules $A \to (x, y)$ and two binary merging rules $A \to [A^l, A^r]$ and $A \to \langle A^l, A^r \rangle$ are allowed.

During decoding, the source language sentence is first divided into phrases (sequence of words), then the lexical translation rule $A \to (x, y)$ translates each source phrase x into target phrase y and forms a block A. The monotone merging rule $A \to [A^l, A^r]$ (or the swap merging rule $A \to \langle A^l, A^r \rangle$) combines the two neighboring blocks into a bigger one until the whole source sentence is covered.

The lexical translation rule $A \to (x, y)$ plays the same role as the phrasal translation pairs (tuples consisting of a source phrase and its target translation hypothesis) in the conventional phrase-based translation models. The monotone merging rule $A \to [A^l, A^r]$ combines the two consecutive blocks into a bigger block by concatenating the two partial target translation candidates in order while the swap rule $A \to \langle A^l, A^r \rangle$ yields the bigger block by swapping the two partial target translation candidates. The probability of the merging rules is estimated using a maximum entropy based algorithm (Xiong et al., 2006).

Similarly, the n-gram language model measures the fluency of the translation outputs. We also apply the same count cutoff pruning technique to figure out the relations between the language model size and the BTG-based translation quality. Table 2 reports the statistics of the baseline n-gram models. The trend is very similar to that of the phrase-based translation, except that the 5-gram model does not outperform significantly over the 4-gram model. In order to keep consistency, we also use the 5-gram model as our baseline for language model pruning.

Table 2. Performance of the BTG-based translation with each n-gram language model

Language Model	Size(MB)	BLEU	Perplexity
Unigram	32	24.29	1155.74
Bigram	458	29.59	201.90
Trigram	1,063	34.92	121.54
4-gram	2,036	36.56	107.64
5-gram	3,079	36.62	104.69
6-gram	4,046	36.68	103.95
7-gram	4,938	36.72	103.54

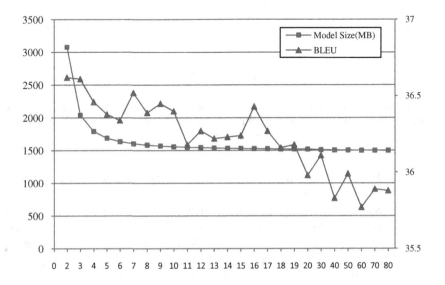

Fig. 2. Performance of BTG-based translation system with pruned language model

Figure 2 gives the statistics of the pruned language model size and the BTG-based translation quality. We can see from the figure that the BTG-based translation system is more sensitive to the count cutoff technique. When the count threshold is bigger than 16, the translation quality decreases rapidly.

2.4   Analysis

The results of pruning imply that the performance of translation can still keep in an acceptable level although the pruned language model is almost only half of the base-line in model size. It sheds new lights to training the language model in practical use. We compare the baseline language model (Table 3) with the pruned one using the threshold value 8, which perform well both in the phrase-based model and BTG-based model, to look into the pruned results in detail.

Table 3. Comparsion between original model and pruned model

N-gram in language model	Baseline	Pruned(threshold value=8)
Unigram	1,715,898	1,715,898
Bigram	16,680,196	16,680,196
Trigram	18,185,555	14,111,461
4-gram	24,364,923	16,234,025
5-gram	25,065,466	1,811,926

Table 3 demonstrates that most part of 5-grams, nearly one third of 4-grams and one fifth of trigrams have been discarded during pruning. Pruning the 5-grams only can also affect the lower order n-grams. This is because during the count cutoff pruning process, the Kneser-Ney smoothing method would modify the lower n-grams (4-grams and trigrams) which the pruned 5-grams are related to.

In general, the performance trends of the two different translation systems are similar with each other and it is consistent with our intuitions. Due to the different translation generation styles, the bottom-up BTG-based translation system is more sensitive to the count threshold compared with the left-to-right phrase-based translation system. We believe it is because that the reordering model in the BTG-based translation system is more powerful than that in the phrase-based system, and the strong reordering model alleviates the dependence on the higher order n-gram language model. However, we will explore the deep reasons in the future work.

According to our analysis, we find another interesting phenomenon: in the pruned language model, many 4-grams and 5-grams share the same trigram which has high relative probability. For example, considering the trigram "*is aimed at*", many 4-grams and 5-grams sharing the same context are shown in Figure 3.

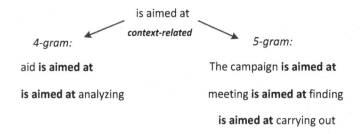

Fig. 3. The trigram "*is aimed at*" is shared in many 4-grams and 5-grams. This figure illustrates some examples.

For better understanding, we further sort all the trigrams by probability in descending order and select the top k frequent trigrams to see how many higher order 4-grams and 5-grams share these frequent trigrams in the pruned language model.   We report the statistics in Table 4.

Table 4. Influence of the top k frequent trigrams in the pruned model. According to statistics in this table, the top 3 million frequent trigrams can cover 41.88% 4-grams and 70.26% 5-grams. The top 5 million frequent trigrams can account for 66.30% 4-grams and 91.11% 5-grams.

k (million)	4-gram	5-gram
1	14.45%	30.97%
2	27.75%	53.27%
3	41.88%	70.26%
4	55.11%	82.98%
5	66.30%	91.11%
6	75.57%	96.24%
7	82.48%	98.51%
8	87.65%	99.39%
9	91.38%	99.69%
10	94.06%	99.86%
>10	>95%	>99.86%

As we can see, the most 4-grams and 5-grams in the pruned language model can be explained with the frequent trigrams. This inspires us to make full use of the frequent trigrams so that we can safely discard all the 4-grams and 5-grams to keep the language model size as small as possible.

3   Frequent Trigram Based Model Pruning

According to our analysis, the frequent trigrams can cover most of the 4-grams and 5-grams. It is natural that we can take full advantage of the frequent trigrams in the language model pruning task.

The idea of capturing the frequent trigram information is not to select the particular n-grams from the language model, but to regard the frequent trigrams as basic language units. Thus, we can treat 4-grams and 5-grams as the new bigram and trigrams related to the original frequent trigrams.

From another point of view, the standard n-gram language model uses the word as the basic unit, and the trigram model can only depict dependence among three words. However, considering the frequent trigrams as basic units, we can capture some relationship in the phrase level. Taking the following English sentence as an example:

The China's policy is aimed at the trade

We find that the phrases '*the China's policy*' and '*is aimed at*' are two frequent trigrams. Therefore, different from the standard word-based trigram language model, we can estimate the probability of this sentence using the new trigram model as below:

$$p(s) = p(\textbf{\textit{the\_china's\_policy}} \mid \text{<s>})*$$

$$p(\textit{is\_aimed\_at} \mid \textbf{\textit{the\_China's\_policy}}, \text{<s>})*$$

$$p(\textit{the} \mid \textbf{\textit{is\_aimed\_at}}, \textbf{\textit{the\_China's\_policy}})*$$

$$p(\textit{trade} \mid \textbf{\textit{the\_China's\_policy}}, \quad \textit{the})*$$

$$p(\text{<s>} \mid \textit{the} , \textit{trade})$$

By using the above new trigram model, we can fill some gap caused by discarding all the baseline 4-grams and 5-grams. However, it still remains a question how to leverage the baseline frequent trigrams in the translation modeling. In this paper, we propose two simple approaches: one treats the frequent trigrams as concrete basic units, and the other cluster the frequent trigrams and learn a variable (cluster) based language model.

3.1 Frequent Trigrams as Concrete Basic Units

Regarding the baseline frequent trigrams as concrete basic units and learning a new trigram model is the same as training a normal language model. The only difference is that we should replace all the recognized frequent trigrams with the basic unit forms. The training procedure can be processed with four steps as follows:

Step 1: extract all trigrams from the pruned language model which performs well in the translation task.

Step 2: sort the trigrams by probability in descending order, and select the top k trigrams as frequent trigrams.

Step 3: find these trigrams in original language model training corpus and replace them with basic unit forms. For Example, "*is aimed at*" is substitute by "*is_aimed_at*". Then we can obtain the new training corpus in which frequent trigrams are transformed into basic units.

Step 4: train the new trigram language model using the new corpus.

During decoding, we incorporate the frequent trigram model as an another language model feature besides the baseline trigram model, into the log-linear model. The total model score is computed by a log-linear combination of a group of translation features, reordering features and the language models.

$$g(h;t,r,lm,lm_f) = w_t \cdot m_t(h) + w_r \cdot m_r(h) + w_{lm} \cdot m_{lm}(h) + w_{lmf} \cdot m_{lmf}(h) \qquad (2)$$

g denotes the total score of the translation hypothesis, t denotes the translation model, r denotes the reordering model, lm denotes the language model and lm_f denotes the new frequent trigram model. w_{lmf} represents the weight of the new frequent trigram model.

When we score a translation hypothesis, we first detect whether there exist frequent trigrams in this hypothesis. When the hypothesis contains the frequent trigrams, we can get a score from new frequent trigram model. We just set the default score of the frequent trigram model 0 in case there is no frequent trigram in the hypothesis.

3.2 Cluster-Based Model

The frequent trigram model can capture much contextual information. According to the property of the frequent trigram model, it can capture similar or more information compared with the baseline 4-grams or 5-grams.

However, the model size will become unacceptable if we retain much more top trigrams. In order to capture the key information and reduce the size of this model, we propose to use the clustering method to capture the patterns in the frequent trigrams. The brown clustering method has been introduced as a pruning method in Section 2. We also use this algorithm as the clustering technique to cluster frequent trigrams rather than single words in the previous work. Intuitively, compared to the frequent trigram model, our cluster-based trigram model will save much storage and will avoid the data sparseness problem.

In order to perform this approach, we directly run brown clustering algorithm on the training corpus which is used for learning the frequent trigram model as we mentioned in the last section. After clustering, we can obtain the classes for each frequent trigram. Then, the training procedure of the clustering model is processed as follows:

Step 1: build a mapping between frequent trigrams and the classes (number).

Step 2: replace the frequent trigrams in the original corpus with class identifier. For instance, we replace "*is aimed at*" with "*C12*".

Step 3: train the new cluster-based language model.

Like the frequent trigram model, we also integrate the cluster-based language model as a new feature into the log-linear translation model besides the baseline trigram model. During decoding, if we detect the frequent trigram in the translation hypothesis, then we replace it with class identifier and retrieve the probability in the cluster-based model.

In addition, we also discard a lot of uninformative n-grams in our cluster-based model, such as:

(a) unigrams in our cluster-based model, because the unigram information is included in the baseline trigram model.
(b) any n-gram containing no frequent trigrams.

4   Experiments and Discussion

We conduct our experiments on NIST Chinese-to-English translation to evaluate the effectiveness of both the frequent trigram language model and the cluster-based model.

To train our baseline trigram language model, the frequent trigram model and the cluster-based trigram model, we use the same corpus and settings as that used in Section 2.

We use the NIST MT03 evaluation test data as the development set, and the NIST MT04, MT05 as the test sets. We also adopt the case-insensitive BLEU-4 with the shortest length penalty as our evaluation metric. The language model size and translation quality results are shown in Table 5.

Table 5. Experimental results of the frequent trigram languge model (flm) and the cluster-based trigram languge model (clm). 4m means use top 4 milion trigrams as the frequent trigrams. 100c means clustering frequent trigrams into 100 word class.

Model	Size(MB)	MT03(dev)	MT04	MT05
Trigram	1000	35.01	34.92	32.95
trigram+flm(4m)	2000	35.60	35.52	33.47
trigram+clm(4m,100c)	1200	35.57	35.50	33.46

From the results in Table 5, we can see that when we combine the frequent trigram language model with the baseline trigram language model, we can obtain significant improvements.

As to the cluster-based trigram language model, it performs similar to the frequent trigram language model, but it can reduce the model size significantly. Specifically, the cluster-based trigram language model outperforms the baseline trigram model with an improvement more than 0.5 BLEU score, while increasing only 200MB storage. It demonstrates the effectiveness of our proposed cluster-based language model.

We have also tried 4-gram model and 5-gram model as our baselines. However, the improvement obtained by the frequent trigram model and the cluster-based language model is not significant. We believe the reason is that the 4-grams and 5-grams contain most information of the new models. Another reason can be seen from Section 2 that with the n-gram order becomes higher, the improvement becomes smaller and smaller.

5   Conclusions and Future Work

This paper presents an investigation about the relations between the language model size and the translation quality in statistical machine translation. Based on our interesting findings, we further propose to replace the higher order n-grams (4-grams and 5-grams) with a low-order (trigram) cluster-based language model which attempts to make full use of the frequent trigrams. The extensive experiments show that our methods are very effective in both of reducing the language model size and improving the translation quality.

In the future, we will study further the frequent trigrams and find more effective algorithms which can capture the intrinsic structure of the language model.

Acknowledgment. The authors are grateful to *International Science & Technology Cooperation Program of China* (Grant No.2014DFA11350) and *High New Technology Research and Development Program of Xinjiang Uyghur Autonomous Region* (Grant No. 201312103).

References

1. Brown, P., Della Pietra, V., de Souza, P., Lai, J., Mercer, R.: Class-based n-gram models of natural language. Computational Linguistics (18), 467–479 (1990)
2. Goodman, J., Gao, J.: Language model size reduction by pruning and clustering. In: Processings of ICSLP 2000, pp. 110–113 (2000)
3. Jelinek, F., Merialdo, B., Roukos, S., Strauss, M.: Self Organized Language modeling for Speech Recognition. In: Waibel, A., Lee, K.F. (eds.) Reading in Speech Recognition. Morgan Kaufmann (1990)
4. Koehn, P., Hoang, H., Birch, A., Callsion-Burch, C., et al.: Moses: Open Source Toolkit for Statistical Machine Translation. In: Proceedings of ACL, pp. 177–180 (2007)
5. Moore, R.C., Quirk, C.: Less is More: Significance-Based N-gram Selection for Smaller, Better Language Models. In: Proceedings of the 2009 Conference on Empirical Methods in Natural Language Processing, pp. 746–755 (2009)
6. Och, F.J.: GIZA++:Training of statistical translation models (2000)
7. http://www-i6.informatik.rwth-aachen.de/~och/software/GIZA++.html
8. Seymore, K., Rosenfeld, R.: Scalable Trigram Backoff Language Models. In: Proceedings of ICSLP 1996, pp. 232–235 (1996)
9. Stolcke, A.: Entropy-based pruning of backoff language model. In: Proceedings of the DARPA News Transcription and Understanding Workshop 1998, pp. 270–274 (1998)
10. Wu, D.: Stochastic inversion transduction grammars and bilingual parsing of parallel corpora. Computational Linguistic 23(3), 377–403 (1997)
11. Xiong, D., Liu, Q., Lin, S.: Maximum entropy based phrase reordering model for statistical machine translation. In: Proceedings of COLING-ACL 2006, pp. 521–528 (2006)
12. Zhang, J., Zong, C.: A Framework for Effectively Integrating Hard and Soft Syntactic Rules into Phrase-Based Translation. In: Proceedings of the 23rd Pacific Asia Conference on Language, Information and Computation (PACLIC 23), Hong Kong, pp. 579–588 (2009)

Data Selection via Semi-supervised Recursive Autoencoders for SMT Domain Adaptation

Yi Lu, Derek F. Wong, Lidia S. Chao, and Longyue Wang

Natural Language Processing & Portuguese-Chinese Machine Translation Laboratory,
Department of Computer and Information Science,
University of Macau, Macau, China
takamachi660@gmail.com, {derekfw,lidiasc}@umac.mo,
vincentwang0229@hotmail.com

Abstract. In this paper, we present a novel data selection approach based on semi-supervised recursive autoencoders. The model is trained to capture the domain specific features and used for detecting sentences, which are relevant to a specific domain, from a large general-domain corpus. The selected data are used for adapting the built language model and translation model to target domain. Experiments were conducted on an in-domain (IWSLT2014 Chinese-English TED Talk) and a general-domain corpus (UM-Corpus). We evaluated the proposed data selection model in both intrinsic and extrinsic evaluations to investigate the selection successful rate (F-score) of pseudo data, as well as the translation quality (BLEU score) of adapting SMT systems. Empirical results reveal the proposed approach outperforms the state-of-the-art selection approach.

Keywords: Statistical Machine Translation, Domain Adaptation, Data Selection, Semi-Supervise, Recursive Autoencoders.

1 Introduction

The translation quality of statistical machine translation (SMT) [2] system heavily depends on the quantity of training data. However, the larger training data is not guaranteed to yield better translation system if the data of training and testing are not identically distributed [23]. In practice, training data directly relevant to the target domain is always insufficient.

A conventional solution is to select appropriate data for the target domain from a large general corpus, which covers several domains as well as the target domain. Then a domain-adapted SMT system can be trained on the selected pseudo in-domain sub-corpus [1] instead of the whole general corpus. The task of data selection is focused on scoring and filtering. Scoring is to estimate the relevance of each sentence or sentence pair S_i in general monolingual or parallel corpus G to the target domain. It can be stated as follows [25]:

$$Score(S_i) \rightarrow Sim(S_i, R) \tag{1}$$

X. Shi and Y. Chen (Eds.): CWMT 2014, CCIS 493, pp. 13–23, 2014.
© Springer-Verlag Berlin Heidelberg 2014

where R is the abstract representation of the target domain model. After scoring, sentence or sentence pair that given a high score will be extracted to form the pseudo in-domain sub-corpus G_{sub}.

It is obvious that the similarity metric heavily impacts the relevance of the selected sub-corpus, and affects the performance of the domain adapted SMT system. Several criteria and techniques have been explored, this includes the use of information retrieval techniques [7, 11, 27], perplexity-based approaches [1,6,14,16], and Levenshtein distance [13,25] for ranking the relevance of domain sentences.

These models mainly rely on the word occurrences (or collocations) to measure the similarities of sentences and usually do not consider the structural information of sentences. As a result, they may fail to learn more useful information to define domains.

In this paper, we propose a data selection framework based on semi-supervised recursive autoencoders (RAE) [19] for measuring the relevance of domain data, which has been proven to be effective for sentiment distribution predicting. RAE is adapted to learn vector representations of phrases and even the entire sentences as well as their tree structures from plain text in an unsupervised manner while capturing the distribution of domain information, i.e. label, at each inter structure of the tree. A classifier is then trained on the vector representations, which could be seen as the features of sentences.

The proposed method was evaluated in terms of both intrinsic and extrinsic metrics that compared with a popular perplexity-based method described by Moore and Lewis [16] on Chinese-English corpora. For the extrinsic evaluation, we applied the selected sub-corpus for language model (LM) and translation model (TM) optimization by combining the models trained on in-domain and selected pseudo in-domain sub-corpus. The translation quality of the built system was evaluated on the Chinese-English translation pair using BLEU [18] metric. We also examine the accuracy of the data selection models by precious, recall, and F measure. In such intrinsic evaluation as well as extrinsic evaluation, the proposed method achieves better performance.

The remainder of this paper is organized as follows. We firstly review the related work in Sect. 2. The proposed and method is described in Sect. 3. Then Sect. 4 details the setup of experiments and reports the evaluation results. Finally, we draw the conclusions in Sect. 5.

2   Related Works

The earliest data selection method is cosine TF-IDF similarity. It is widely used in many applications of information retrieval (IR) realm such as search engines. This IR technique is applied by Hildebrand et al. [7] to select small but more domain relevant corpus for TM and LM optimization. This standard IR methods considers only keywords overlap, thus it may be weak in removing irrelevant data.

The most popular selection criterion is the perplexity-based method, which is firstly utilized in the field of language modeling by Lin et al. [14] and Gao et al. [6].

More recently, Moore and Lewis [16] used cross-entropy difference which involves an in-domain LM and out-domain LM to calculate the score of text segments. The ranking of the sentences in general corpus using perplexity was applied to MT by Yasuda et al. [26] and Foster et al. [5]. Axelrod et al. [1] further extended perplexity-based model to bilingual application and employed these perplexity-based method variants for SMT domain adaptation and improved the scores by 1.8 BLEU points while discarding more than 99% of training data. In general, the modified Moore-Lewis (bilingual cross-entropy difference) model achieves better overall performance than IR methods and other perplexity-based variants, thus it is often used in the tasks of domain adaptation.

The perplexity of a string s with empirical n-gram distribution p, given a language model q is:

$$2^{H(p,q)} = 2^{-\sum_x p(x) \log q(x)} \tag{2}$$

in which $H(p,q)$ is the cross-entropy between p and q. And the similarity between s and target domain can be calculated by cross-entropy difference [16]:

$$score(s) = H_I(s) - H_O(s) \tag{3}$$

where the $H_I(s)$ and $H_O(s)$ are the cross-entropy between the string s and an in-domain language model LM_I and an out-domain LM_O respectively trained on in-domain data and out-domain data.

In this study, we compare our proposed model with Moore-Lewis since it shows outstanding performance. Another perplexity-based variant, modified Moore-Lewis is not compared because it is grounded in the bilingual setting.

Another data selection method is edit-distance [13], which has been widely used as similarity measure for translation memory and example-based MT (EBMT). Koehn and Senellart [10] applied this method to retrieve translation template from a translation memory and then used SMT system to translate the unmatched part in the sentences. Leveling et al. [12] investigated several approximated sentence retrieval methods including edit-distance for EBMT. This selection method was recently applied for domain adaptation and the results showed that it works well if the general corpus contains sentences that are very close to the in-domain dataset [25].

3   Proposed Method

The workflow of our proposed data selection model is illustrated in Fig. 1. Firstly, we learn a RAE model in a semi-supervised manner using in-domain and out-domain training data. This model is used for extracting features from sentences of the training data, i.e. transforming sentences into their vector representations. Then a simple logistic regression can be trained on the (vector, domain label) pairs. To predict the label of unlabeled data, vectors representing the new sentences are obtained by applying the RAE model and determined by the classifier. The score for each sentence is defined as the weight on the in-domain class calculated by the classifier. We detail the proposed method in the remaining part of this section.

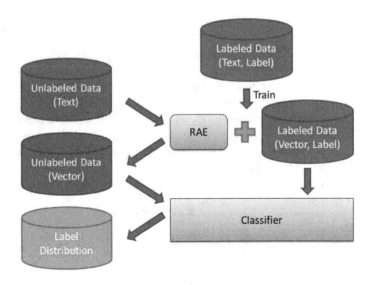

Fig. 1. Workflow of proposed data selection model

The recursive autoencoders [19] aim to transfer variable-sized phrases as well as the entire sentence into vector space representations (also known as embedding), without given tree structure. As the beginning, each word vector is initialized by sampling from a zero mean Gaussian distribution. Then a greedy unsupervised RAE algorithm is used for predicting tree structure according to the reconstruction error:

$$E_{rec}([c_1; c_2]) = \frac{||[c_1; c_2] - [c'_1; c'_2]||^2}{2} \tag{4}$$

where c_i and c'_i are the child nodes and the corresponding ones in the reconstruction layer of a non-terminal node p (Fig. 2). Let n_i be the number of words underneath c_i, the reconstruction error can be adjusted as follow in order to increase the importance of the child which represent higher number of collapsed words:

$$E_{rec}([c_1; c_2]) = \frac{n_1}{n_1 + n_2}||c_1 - c'_1||^2 + \frac{n_2}{n_1 + n_2}||c_2 - c'_2||^2 \tag{5}$$

Let $A(x)$ be all possible trees that can be built from an input sentence x, the best tree y can be found by:

$$RAE_\theta(x) = \arg\min_{y \in A(x)} \sum_p E_{rec}([c_1; c_2]_p) \tag{6}$$

In order to capture the phrase and sentence level label distribution, the unsupervised RAE is extended to a semi-supervised setting. The vector associated to each node of the tree built by the RAE could be seen as features describing

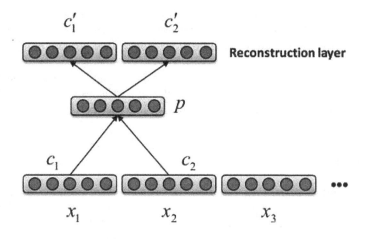

Fig. 2. Illustration of reconstruction layer

that phrase and could be leveraged by adding a simple softmax layer on top of it for predicting the label distributions:

$$d(p; \theta) = \text{softmax}(W^{label}p) \tag{7}$$

As we have two labels (in-domain and out-domain), $d \in \mathbb{R}^2$ is a 2-dimensional multinomial distribution and $d_{in} + d_{out} = 1$. Let t_k be the kth element of the multinomial target label distribution t for one sentence. The cross-entropy error can be defined as:

$$E_{ce}(p, t; \theta) = -\sum_{k=1}^{2} t_k \log d_k(p; \theta) \tag{8}$$

Combining reconstruction error and cross-entropy error, the error at each non-terminal node is the weighted sum:

$$E([c_1; c_2]_p, p, t; \theta) = \alpha E_{rec}([c_1; c_2]_p; \theta) + (1 - \alpha)E_{ce}(p, t; \theta) \tag{9}$$

The error for each (sentence, label) pair (x, t) is the sum over the error at the nodes of the tree from (6):

$$E(x, t; \theta) = \sum_{p \in RAE_\theta(x)} E([c_1; c_2]_p, p, t; \theta) \tag{10}$$

Then the final semi-supervised RAE objective becomes

$$J = \frac{1}{N} \sum_{(x,t)} E(x, t; \theta) + \frac{\lambda}{2}||\theta||^2 \tag{11}$$

The hyperparameter α trade-off the reconstruction error and cross-entropy error parts of the objective and influences the performance. In this task, we consider that it is important to give more weight to the supervised objective in order to capture the label distribution.

In order to measure the domain relevance of a sentence with this model, we use the vector representations of the root nodes of sentences learned from RAE to train a simple logistic regression classifier, and treat the resulting weight of the in-domain class as the relevance score.

4 Experiments

As Moore-Lewis data selection is reported the most effective method, we compare this strong method with our proposed model. For Moore-Lewis, we implement it based on n-gram language model, SRILM toolkit[1] [20]. For RAE-based word representation model and classifier, we apply an open-source toolkit[2] with default settings. We apply the RAE and Moore-Lewis to score each sentence or sentence pairs in general-domain corpus. Then select them to adapt language model and translation model (in Sect. 4.3).

4.1 Corpora

The task of domain adaptation requires two corpora. The in-domain corpus and test set are IWSLT2014 (International Workshop on Spoken Language Translation) Chinese-English TED Talk and IWSLT dev2010 [3]. We used UM-Corpus [21] as general corpus. It comprises various genres such as news, spoken, laws, thesis, education, science, subtitle, and microblog. Such a rich general corpus brings more challenges to the data selection criterion. The spoken part of UM-Corpus is considered as good candidate for pseudo in-domain sub-corpus. Task oriented pre-processing [15, 22] is applied to in-domain training set and general corpus. In preprocessing, the Chinese texts are segmented using a CRFs based toolkit[3] [24]. Both Moore-Lewis and RAE models require an out-domain training set. We obtained out-domain training and test set by randomly selecting from the general corpus. The out-domain data sets have the same size as the corresponding in-domain data sets. Sentences of those data sets are disjoint. The statistics information of the out-domain training and test set are summarized in Table 1.

Table 1. Corpora statistics (English side)

Data set	Sentences	Tokens	Vocabulary	Avg. Len.
Out-train	177,477	3,285,197	136,260	18.51
Out-test	887	16,663	4,967	18.79

---

[1] http://www.speech.sri.com/projects/srilm/.

[2] JRAE version rc3 is available at https://github.com/sancha/jrae/.

[3] http://nlp2ct.cis.umac.mo/Tokenizer/tokenizer.jsf.

4.2   Intrinsic Evaluation

The objective of this evaluation is to directly examine the models ability to recognize in-domain sentences. We use the union set of in-domain and out-domain test set (totally 1,774 sentences) as the test set. Since Moore-Lewis can only score the sentence without label prediction, we explore two settings in order to compare it with the proposed method fairly. In the first setting, we obtain the output sentences from the RAE classifier and denote the number of sentences labeled in-domain as N_{In}. Then select top N_{In} sentences ranked by Moore-Lewis model as the in-domain prediction from Moore-Lewis. In the second setting, we sort the score output from both RAE and Moore-Lewis models and select top 887 (half) sentences as their in-domain predictions. Models are evaluated by a standard precision, recall and F1 score metric. The proposed RAE data selection model outperforms Moore-Lewis in both settings. Details are shown in Table 2.

Table 2. Intrinsic Evaluation Results

Setting	N_{In}	Models	Precision	Recall	F1
1st	1,013	RAE	76.01	86.80	81.05
		M-L	69.67	79.89	74.43
2nd	887	RAE	78.75	78.75	78.75
		M-L	70.67	70.90	70.78

4.3   Extrinsic Evaluation

In this sub-section, we report the impacts of selection approaches on the domain-specific translation quality. To build a SMT system, we employ the state-of-the-art SMT toolkit, Moses 1.0[4] [8] as decoder. The translation and re-ordering model utilizes the grow-diag-final symmetrized word-to-word alignments created with Fast Align[5] [4]. A 5-gram language model is trained using SRILM with improved modified Kneser-Ney smoothing, and quantizing both probabilities and back-off weights. Finally the minimum-error-rate training (MERT) [17] is taken for tuning the parameters.

The top M percentages of ranked sentences are selected, where $M=\{10, 20, 30, 40, 50, 60, 70, 80, 90\}$. Then we carried out the experiments for LM and TM optimization separately using the selected pseudo in-domain data, and aims to evaluate the effectiveness of the proposed approach against the Moore-Lewis data selection method.

Language Model Adaptation. We trained additional 5-grams LMs for different M sizes of data and interpolated it with in-domain to construct the enhanced systems. The absolute BLEU scores of the evaluated systems are shown in Fig. 3. RAE performs best when $M=50$, indicating that it does successfully reduce the

---

[4] http://www.statmt.org/moses/.
[5] https://github.com/clab/fast_align/.

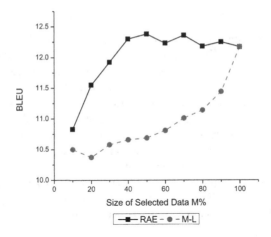

Fig. 3. Evaluation results for systems that enhanced with additional LMs

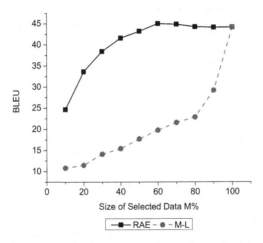

Fig. 4. Evaluation results for systems that enhanced with additional TMs

noise from the general corpus, while the systems enhanced by Moore-Lewis cannot outperform the system trained on the entire general corpus (M=100) at any experimented point of M.

Translation Model Adaptation. Additional TMs (phrase tables) for different M values were trained and log-linearly interpolated with the in-domain model using the multi-decoding method described by Koehn and Schroeder [9]. The trend of the evaluation results (Fig. 4) is quite similar to the result of LM optimization. RAE outperforms Moore-Lewis significantly and makes maximum improvement when M=60. To further analyze the results, we inspected the sub-corpus selected by these two models and counted the number of common sentences selected by both methods. There are around 54.5% of sentences in the sub-corpus produced by the two methods when M=60. This number declines to 2.93% when M goes to 10.

5 Conclusion

In this paper, we treat data selection problem as scoring the sentences in a general corpus and present a new selection approach which is based on semi-supervised recursive autoencoders. We compare it with the most promising Moore-Lewis data selection model and evaluate them in two ways. In the evaluations, we firstly examine the models ability to retrieve the in-domain sentences from a standard test set which includes equally sized in-domain and out-domain sentences. Then we apply the selection methods to a real domain adaptation task in which we extract sub-corpus from a general corpus to boost the performance of domain-specific SMT system. The results of these two evaluation show positive correlation. Our RAE method outperforms Moore-Lewis in both evaluation and gains large improvement (by 26.15 BLEU scores at most) in the translation model optimization task. We conclude that semi-supervised RAE is a suitable data selection model for SMT domain adaptation task although it is more complicated to construct and requires more computation and memory resources.

Acknowledgements. The authors are grateful to the Science and Technology Development Fund of Macau and the Research Committee of the University of Macau for the funding support for their research, under the Reference nos. MYRG076 (Y1-L2)-FST13-WF and MYRG070 (Y1-L2)-FST12-CS.

References

1. Axelrod, A., He, X., Gao, J.: Domain adaptation via pseudo in-domain data selection. In: Proceedings of the Conference on Empirical Methods in Natural Language Processing, pp. 355–362. Association for Computational Linguistics (2011)
2. Brown, P.F., Pietra, V.J.D., Pietra, S.A.D., Mercer, R.L.: The mathematics of statistical machine translation: Parameter estimation. Computational Linguistics 19(2), 263–311 (1993)
3. Cettolo, M., Girardi, C., Federico, M.: Wit3: Web inventory of transcribed and translated talks. In: Proceedings of the 16th Conference of the European Association for Machine Translation (EAMT), pp. 261–268 (2012)
4. Dyer, C., Chahuneau, V., Smith, N.A.: A simple, fast, and effective reparameterization of IBM model 2. In: HLT-NAACL, pp. 644–648. Citeseer (2013)
5. Foster, G., Goutte, C., Kuhn, R.: Discriminative instance weighting for domain adaptation in statistical machine translation. In: Proceedings of the 2010 Conference on Empirical Methods in Natural Language Processing, pp. 451–459. Association for Computational Linguistics (2010)

6. Gao, J., Goodman, J., Li, M., Lee, K.F.: Toward a unified approach to statistical language modeling for chinese. ACM Transactions on Asian Language Information Processing (TALIP) 1(1), 3–33 (2002)
7. Hildebrand, A.S., Eck, M., Vogel, S., Waibel, A.: Adaptation of the translation model for statistical machine translation based on information retrieval. In: Proceedings of EAMT, vol. 2005, pp. 133–142 (2005)
8. Koehn, P., Hoang, H., Birch, A., Callison-Burch, C., Federico, M., Bertoldi, N., Cowan, B., Shen, W., Moran, C., Zens, R., et al.: Moses: Open source toolkit for statistical machine translation. In: Proceedings of the 45th Annual Meeting of the ACL on Interactive Poster and Demonstration Sessions, pp. 177–180. Association for Computational Linguistics (2007)
9. Koehn, P., Schroeder, J.: Experiments in domain adaptation for statistical machine translation. In: Proceedings of the Second Workshop on Statistical Machine Translation, pp. 224–227. Association for Computational Linguistics (2007)
10. Koehn, P., Senellart, J.: Convergence of translation memory and statistical machine translation. In: Proceedings of AMTA Workshop on MT Research and the Translation Industry, pp. 21–31 (2010)
11. Lü, Y., Huang, J., Liu, Q.: Improving statistical machine translation performance by training data selection and optimization. In: EMNLP-CoNLL, pp. 343–350. Citeseer (2007)
12. Leveling, J., Ganguly, D., Dandapat, S., Jones, G.J.: Approximate sentence retrieval for scalable and efficient example-based machine translation (2012)
13. Levenshtein, V.I.: Binary codes capable of correcting deletions, insertions and reversals. Soviet Physics Doklady 10, 707 (1966)
14. Lin, S.C., Tsai, C.L., Chien, L.F., Chen, K.J., Lee, L.S.: Chinese language model adaptation based on document classification and multiple domain-specific language models. In: Fifth European Conference on Speech Communication and Technology (1997)
15. Lu, Y., Wang, L., Wong, D.F., Chao, L.S., Wang, Y., Oliveira, F.: Domain adaptation for medical text translation using web resources. In: ACL 2014, p. 233 (2014)
16. Moore, R.C., Lewis, W.: Intelligent selection of language model training data. In: Proceedings of the ACL 2010 Conference Short Papers, pp. 220–224. Association for Computational Linguistics (2010)
17. Och, F.J.: Minimum error rate training in statistical machine translation. In: Proceedings of the 41st Annual Meeting on Association for Computational Linguistics, vol. 1, pp. 160–167. Association for Computational Linguistics (2003)
18. Papineni, K., Roukos, S., Ward, T., Zhu, W.J.: BLEU: a method for automatic evaluation of machine translation. In: Proceedings of the 40th Annual Meeting on Association for Computational Linguistics, pp. 311–318. Association for Computational Linguistics (2002)
19. Socher, R., Pennington, J., Huang, E.H., Ng, A.Y., Manning, C.D.: Semi-supervised recursive autoencoders for predicting sentiment distributions. In: Proceedings of the Conference on Empirical Methods in Natural Language Processing, pp. 151–161. Association for Computational Linguistics (2011)
20. Stolcke, A.: others: SRILM-an extensible language modeling toolkit. In: INTERSPEECH (2002)
21. Tian, L., Wong, D., Chao, L., Quaresma, P., Oliveira, F., Lu, Y., Li, S., Wang, Y., Wang, L.: UM-corpus: a large english-chinese parallel corpus for statistical machine translation. In: Proceedings of the 9th International Conference on Language Resources and Evaluation (2014)

22. Wang, L., Lu, Y., Wong, D.F., Chao, L.S., Wang, Y., Oliveira, F.: Combining domain adaptation approaches for medical text translation. In: ACL 2014, p. 254 (2014)
23. Wang, L., Wong, D.F., Chao, L.S., Lu, Y., Xing, J.: A systematic comparison of data selection criteria for SMT domain adaptation. The Scientific World Journal 2014 (2014)
24. Wang, L., Wong, D.F., Chao, L.S., Xing, J.: CRFs-based chinese word segmentation for micro-blog with small-scale data. In: Proceedings of the Second CIPS-SIGHAN Joint Conference on Chinese Language, pp. 51–57. Citeseer (2012)
25. Wang, L., Wong, D.F., Chao, L.S., Xing, J., Lu, Y., Trancoso, I.: Edit distance: A new data selection criterion for domain adaptation in SMT. In: RANLP, pp. 727–732 (2013)
26. Yasuda, K., Zhang, R., Yamamoto, H., Sumita, E.: Method of selecting training data to build a compact and efficient translation model. In: IJCNLP, pp. 655–660 (2008)
27. Zhao, B., Eck, M., Vogel, S.: Language model adaptation for statistical machine translation with structured query models. In: Proceedings of the 20th International Conference on Computational Linguistics, p. 411. Association for Computational Linguistics (2004)

Effective Hypotheses Re-ranking Model in Statistical Machine Translation

Yiming Wang, Longyue Wang, Derek F. Wong, and Lidia S. Chao

Natural Language Processing & Portuguese-Chinese Machine Translation Laboratory,
Department of Computer and Information Science,
University of Macau, Macau, China
wang2008499@gmail.com, vincentwang0229@hotmail.com,
{derekfw,lidiasc}@umac.mo

Abstract. In statistical machine translation, an effective way to improve the translation quality is to regularize the posterior probabilities of translation hypotheses according to the information of N-best list. In this paper, we present a novel approach to improve the final translation result by dynamically augmenting the translation scores of hypotheses that derived from the N-best translation candidates. The proposed model was trained on a general domain UM-Corpus and evaluated on IWSLT Chinese-English TED Talk data under the configurations of *document level* translation and *sentence level* translation respectively. Empirical results real that sentence level translation model outperforms the document level and the baseline system.

Keywords: Phrase-Based Machine Translation, N-best List, Hypotheses Re-Ranking, Hypotheses Re-decoding.

1 Introduction

Decoding is an essential part in statistical machine translation (SMT) [3,4,9,18], however, decoding algorithms are intractable and usually suffer from slow decoding time due to the large search space. Pruning is commonly meant to minimize the search space, while it also drops lots of high quality hypotheses before all words in source sentence have been translated. High quality translation phrases may be discarded because of the scoring function [21,25,28]. A series of methods have been proposed to re-cover the final translation using hypotheses in the N-best list.

Combination of the outputs from different translation systems is firstly adopted to boost the final translation result by using the different level of translation hypotheses, i.e. words, phrases, even sentences [10,20]. The translation cost of those hypotheses are re-estimated from the candidates from multiple translation systems. The hypotheses are used to search a better path for final translation in the re-decoding phase. Transductive learning model [26] enhances the translation system by repeatedly training the system with additional N-best translation hypotheses from the development and test sets. It shows the translation model can

X. Shi and Y. Chen (Eds.): CWMT 2014, CCIS 493, pp. 24–32, 2014.

be improved by using the information in N-best list. Chen et al., [2] exploit the use of N-best hypotheses to self-enhance the probabilities of the translation phrases. Similar to Ueffing et al. [26], the enhancement process was carried out repeatedly using the generated N-best list to improve the overall performance of a SMT system. All these approaches are based on the use of N-best translation lists to boost the final translation in the second pass. Consensus decoding is proposed based on single and multiple systems: single-based method [5,12,13,24] re-ranks the translation results generated by a single system using n-gram posteriors or expected n-gram counts, while it gets a small improvement because of the correlated of the N-best hypotheses in a single system. Extended works have been made on multiple systems [6,7,15]. Final translation result is selected from the combined hypotheses according to the posterior distributions of every system. Though it enhances the improvement from this post-processing, the search space in decoding remains the same. Hypotheses mixture decoding [8] addresses this problem by using alternative decoding scheme to reconstruct the hypotheses of different structure generated by different translation systems, i.e. phrase-based and tree-based models where the translation hypotheses are of different representations. However, all of these methods use hypotheses from multiple models. There is very few study in exploring the use of internal knowledge of a single model. We believe even a model that trained on such a large parallel corpus has already been equipped with good hypotheses. Second, we found that existing studies usually investigate on using a small N-best candidates in selecting the best translation. High quality hypotheses might be ignored. Thus, another objective of this study aims to answer the question if we can recover good and infrequency translation hypotheses from a large set of candidates.

This paper proposes dynamic hypotheses re-ranking model. It is a two-pass decoding strategy based on the standard Maximum a Posterior decoding scheme. In the first pass, an N-best list of translation candidates are generated from the test set. Probabilities $\varphi(e|f)$ of hypotheses[1] derived from the N-best list are re-estimated. In this framework, extracted hypotheses serve as the search space for decoding in the second pass.

The remainder of this paper is organized as follows: Section 2 gives the details of our proposed method. Section 3 describes the experiments and evaluation methods. Section 4 presents the results and discussions, followed by conclusions and future work.

2   Proposed Method

The direct phrase translation probability in phrase table plays an important role as it effects the quality of translation result. Some good hypotheses are usually pruned to limit the space for searching. Hence, the information extracted from N-best list can be treated as an important source to affect the translation probability. In this study, we propose of extracting the translation phrase-pairs from

---

[1] In this paper, translation hypothesis is used to represent a translation word-, phrase- and sentence-pair.

hypotheses and augment the reconstructed phrase table for the final translation. The translation probabilities of the derived phrase table are enhanced according to the frequency of phrases from the N-best list. Under this framework, variants of the approach are investigated.

2.1   Document Level Translation

The state-of-the-art decoder uses phrase table for the decoding process. The phrase table is usually employed in a static way, where the probabilities as well as the entries of phrases will not be altered in the translation process. In this study, we dynamically derive the possible translation phrases from the N-best list for the second pass of decoding. Under this framework, the derivation of translation table falls into two situations: document level and sentence level. In document level, the phrase table is constructed based on the translation hypotheses of the input document, and the probabilities of the phrase-pairs are estimated on the whole set of document. In contrast, the translation framework is detailed to an individual sentence. The objective of this setting is to minimize the interference of phrasal distributions among the sentences of the document. The conventional phrase translation probabilities are computed as:

$$p\left(\widetilde{e}|\widetilde{f}\right) = \frac{N_{train}\left(\widetilde{f},\widetilde{e}\right)}{N_{train}\left(\widetilde{f}\right)} \tag{1}$$

where $\widetilde{f}$ and $\widetilde{e}$ are the phrase of source and target languages. $N_{train}(\widetilde{f})$ is the frequencies of the source phrase observed in training data, and $N_{train}(\widetilde{f},\widetilde{e})$ indicates the frequencies of translation phrase-pair, $\left\langle \widetilde{f},\widetilde{e}\right\rangle$, observed in training data. In our model, the translation probabilities are augmented by the extra counts of phrase-pairs retrieved from the translation hypotheses (N-best list):

$$p'\left(\widetilde{e}|\widetilde{f}\right) = p\left(\widetilde{e}|\widetilde{f}\right)[1 + \frac{N_{nbest}\left(\widetilde{f},\widetilde{e}\right)}{N_{nbest}(\widetilde{f})}] \tag{2}$$

where $N_{nbest}(\widetilde{f})$ is the frequencies of a source phrase observed in the N-best list, and $N_{nbest}(\widetilde{f},\widetilde{e})$ represent the number of translation phrases in N-best list. Algorithm 1 presents the translation procedure for document level translation.

2.2   Sentence Level Translation

In document level translation, the reconstructed phrase table is the collection of phrase-pairs derived from all the sentences of the input document. It is unavoidable that the scores of rarely observed phrase-pairs in the N-best list of a sentence will be badly interfered by the highly observed ones that extracted from the rest of document. Hypothetically, we can reinforce the importance of those low frequent translation phrase-pairs to the translation of specific sentence, and minimize the

---

Algorithm 1. Document Level Translation Model

Input:
   Test set T
Run:
   New phrase table Phr
1. **for** sentence $t_i \in T$ **do**
2.   Decode and generate N-best list
3.   Extract translation phrases $\langle \widetilde{f}, \widetilde{e} \rangle$ from N-best list and append them to Phr
4. **end for**
5. Score the translation probabilities $p(\widetilde{f}, \widetilde{e})$ with Equation (2)
6. Translate all sentences, $t_i \in T$ with pseudo phrase table

---

interference that might cause by irrelevant sentences, in particular, when domain specific translation is the concern. On the other hand, the two-pass search strategy is usually adopted for filtering out the bad or irrelevant phrase-pairs, to change the probability space of the translation model. In addition, with the limit translation hypotheses (compact phrase table), we are able to have more rooms for searching a better decoding path for the final translation. Algorithm 2 presents the procedures for sentence level translation approach.

Algorithm 2. Sentence Level Translation Model

Input:
   Test set T
Run:
1. **for** sentence $T_i \in T$ **do**
2.   Decode T_i and generate N-best list
3.   Extract translation phrases $\langle \widetilde{f}, \widetilde{e} \rangle$ from N-best list and use it as new phrase table

4.   Score the translation probabilities $p(\widetilde{e}|\widetilde{f})$ with Equation (2)
5.   Translate t_i with pseudo phrase table
6.   Discard the constructed pseudo phrase table
7. **end for**

In phrase-based model, translation probabilities are estimated using the relative frequencies. However, in Equation (2), the translation probabilities are augmented by a proportional of the phrase-pairs observed from the N-best hypotheses. In some sense, that does not conform to the standard way in computing the translation probabilities. Hence, we also employ the naïve way to score the new constructed phrase table by:

$$p'' \left(\widetilde{e} | \widetilde{f} \right) = \frac{N_{train} \left(\widetilde{f}, \widetilde{e} \right) + N_{nbest} \left(\widetilde{f}, \widetilde{e} \right)}{N_{train} \left(\widetilde{f} \right) + N_{nbest} \left(\widetilde{f} \right)} \tag{3}$$

The intuition is that based on frequencies of original phrase table, high quality phrase-pairs are further reinforced by the frequencies $N_{nbest}(\widetilde{f}, \widetilde{e})$. Different from the model of Chen et al. [2], we do not need to penalize the low quality phrase-pairs. Since the newly constructed phrase table will filter out any poor or irrelevant phrase-pairs from the N-best translations. In particular in the sentence level translation model, the impact is more obvious. Algorithm 3 presents the translation procedure of sentence level model using the revised probabilities estimation method.

Algorithm 3. Sentence Level Translation Model II

Input:
   Test set T
Run:
   1. **for** sentence $T_i \in T$ **do**
   2.   Decoder and generate N-best list
   3.   Extract translation phrases $\langle \widetilde{f}, \widetilde{e} \rangle$ from N-best list and use it as new phrase table

   4.   Score the translation probabilities $p(\widetilde{e}|\widetilde{f})$ with Equation (3)
   5.   Translate t_i with pseudo phrase table
   6.   Discard the constructed pseudo phrase table
   7. **end for**

---

3   Experiments and Setup

The experiments were conducted on Chinese to English IWSLT2014 (International Workshop on Spoken Language Translation) tasks on the TED Talk corpus [1]. We used IWSLT development and evaluation test set as our development set and test set. All evaluated models were trained on the UM-Corpus [23], which is a multi-domain corpus consisting of 2.2 million sentences of various genres such as news, spoken, laws, subtitle, microblog, etc. In preprocessing, the English texts were tokenized using the scripts provided by Moses [11] and the Chinese texts were segmented using an in-house segmentation tool[2] [27] based on CRFs [14]. The statistics summary of the used data is illustrated in Table 1.

Table 1. Statistical summary of used data

	Language	Token	Vocabulary	Sentences	Ave. Len.
UM-Corpus	En	33,742,781	832,518	2,200,000	13.3
	Zh	56,830,161	209,729	2,200,000	22.5
IWSLT-Dev	En	20,124	3,263	887	22.7
	Zh	21.287	3,888	887	23.9
IWSLT-Test	En	32,062	3,806	1,570	20.4

The training environment is executed in a server equipped with a Xeon processor at 2.9GHz, with 192GB physical memory. The experiments were carried

---

[2] http://nlp2ct.cis.umac.mo/Tokenizer/tokenizer.jsf

out with the Moses Toolkit[3] [11] based on a standard log-linear phrase-based SMT model. The word alignment was trained using the GIZA++[4] based on five iterations of IBM model 1, three for IBM models 3 and 4, and five for HMM alignment [17]. The translation and the reordering model relied on "grow-diag-final" symmetrized word-to-word alignments. The weights of the log-linear model were optimized by means of MERT [16]. A 5-gram language model was trained for English using the SRILM Toolkit[5] [22], exploiting improved modified Kneser-Ney smoothing and quantizing both probabilities and back-off weights.

We evaluated our model against the work of Chen et al. [2]. Consider that both of the works adopted similar approach to reinforce the translation model by using the additional phrase-pair frequencies extracted from the N-best candidates. The difference is they attended to fine tune the translation probabilities of phrase table using development data in a static way. Once the tuning is done, the scores will not be altered. In contrast, the tuning of translation model of our approach is carried out dynamically according to the test set, without modifying the scores of the original model. For comparison, four models are selected and implemented:

- **Baseline**: Chen's model is implemented and used as the baseline system;
- $\mathbf{Model_{DL\text{-}A1}}$: document level translation model implemented with Algorithm 1;
- $\mathbf{Model_{SL\text{-}A2}}$: sentence level translation model as described by Algorithm 2;
- $\mathbf{Model_{SL\text{-}A3}}$: alternative sentence level translation model outlined by Algorithm 3.

The size of N-best list was set to 3,000 for all models, as it achieves the best performance reported by Chen et al. [2].

4   Results and Discussions

Table 2 shows the translation quality measured in terms of BLEU metric [19]. We found that the document level translation system $\mathbf{Model_{DL\text{-}A1}}$ did not perform well as we expected. The BLEU scores drop slightly (0.04 BLEU points) compared to the baseline. When we moved to the sentence level translation models, both the $\mathbf{Model_{SL\text{-}A2}}$ and $\mathbf{Model_{SL\text{-}A3}}$ outperform the baseline system, with an improvement of 0.13 and 0.31 BLEU scores respectively, showing that the proposed model when applied to sentence level translation is effective to reinforce the overall performance of the translation model. In particular, when the translation probabilities are estimated using the relative frequencies of phrase-pairs.

When we look into the translation results of the proposed models, it is easy to find that the translation of sentence level models, $\mathbf{Model_{SL}}$ is better than that of the document level one, $\mathbf{Model_{DL}}$. The use of word in target language is

---

[3] http://www.statmt.org/moses
[4] http://www.statmt.org/moses/giza/GIZA++.html
[5] http://www.speech.sri.com/projects/srilm

much better to the topic of the sentence. For example, by inspecting the translation fragment of the following sentence:

Input: ...如果你这些天读了关于中国的经济新闻...

Reference: ... *reading the **economic news** coming out of **China** these days*...

Model$_{DL}$: ... *reading **Chinese economic news**...*

Model$_{SL}$: ... *reading of **China's economic news**...*

The document level model translation the "中国的经济新闻" into "*Chinese economic news*". However, for the sentence level model, the word "中国/China" is properly used instead of "Chinese" in this context. This reveals that using the information from the N-best translation list can improve the overall translation performance.

Table 2. The translation results in terms of BLEU scores

Model	BLEU
Baseline	39.28
Model$_{DL-A1}$	39.24 (-0.04)
Model$_{SL-A2}$	39.41 (+0.13)
Model$_{SL-A3}$	39.59 (+0.31)

5   Conclusion and Future Work

In this paper, we describe an alternative approach to boost the final translation performance by using the information of N-best hypotheses given by the translation model itself. Two variants of model, document and sentence level translation, are derived and evaluated on the ISWLT 2014 tasks on the TED Talk corpus. The models were trained on a multi-domain UM-Corpus. Empirical results demonstrated that the proposed model on sentence level translation outperforms the baseline system and the document level translation model. Different from existing approaches, the model uses only the internal knowledge of a single model. In future, we may consider of extending this model to use the N-best lists from multiple translation systems.

Acknowledgements. The authors are grateful to the Science and Technology Development Fund of Macau and the Research Committee of the University of Macau for the funding support for their research, under the Reference nos. MYRG076 (Y1-L2)-FST13-WF and MYRG070 (Y1-L2)-FST12-CS.

References

1. Cettolo, M., Girardi, C., Federico, M.: Wit3: Web inventory of transcribed and translated talks. In: Proceedings of the 16th Conference of the European Association for Machine Translation (EAMT), pp. 261–268 (2012)
2. Chen, B., Zhang, M., Aw, A., Li, H.: Exploiting n-best hypotheses for smt self-enhancement. In: Proceedings of the 46th Annual Meeting of the Association for Computational Linguistics on Human Language Technologies: Short Papers, pp. 157–160. Association for Computational Linguistics (2008)
3. Chiang, D.: A hierarchical phrase-based model for statistical machine translation. In: Proceedings of the 43rd Annual Meeting on Association for Computational Linguistics, pp. 263–270. Association for Computational Linguistics (2005)
4. Chiang, D.: Learning to translate with source and target syntax. In: Proceedings of the 48th Annual Meeting of the Association for Computational Linguistics, pp. 1443–1452. Association for Computational Linguistics (2010)
5. DeNero, J., Chiang, D., Knight, K.: Fast consensus decoding over translation forests. In: Proceedings of the Joint Conference of the 47th Annual Meeting of the ACL and the 4th International Joint Conference on Natural Language Processing of the AFNLP, vol. 2, pp. 567–575. Association for Computational Linguistics (2009)
6. DeNero, J., Kumar, S., Chelba, C., Och, F.: Model combination for machine translation. In: Human Language Technologies: The 2010 Annual Conference of the North American Chapter of the Association for Computational Linguistics, pp. 975–983. Association for Computational Linguistics (2010)
7. Duan, N., Li, M., Zhang, D., Zhou, M.: Mixture model-based minimum bayes risk decoding using multiple machine translation systems. In: Proceedings of the 23rd International Conference on Computational Linguistics, pp. 313–321. Association for Computational Linguistics (2010)
8. Duan, N., Li, M., Zhou, M.: Hypothesis mixture decoding for statistical machine translation. In: Proceedings of the 49th Annual Meeting of the Association for Computational Linguistics: Human Language Technologies, vol. 1, pp. 1258–1267. Association for Computational Linguistics (2011)
9. Galley, M., Graehl, J., Knight, K., Marcu, D., DeNeefe, S., Wang, W., Thayer, I.: Scalable inference and training of context-rich syntactic translation models. In: Proceedings of the 21st International Conference on Computational Linguistics and the 44th Annual Meeting of the Association for Computational Linguistics, pp. 961–968. Association for Computational Linguistics (2006)
10. Huang, F., Papineni, K.: Hierarchical system combination for machine translation. In: EMNLP-CoNLL, pp. 277–286. Citeseer (2007)
11. Koehn, P., Hoang, H., Birch, A., Callison-Burch, C., Federico, M., Bertoldi, N., Cowan, B., Shen, W., Moran, C., Zens, R., et al.: Moses: Open source toolkit for statistical machine translation. In: Proceedings of the 45th Annual Meeting of the ACL on Interactive Poster and Demonstration Sessions, pp. 177–180. Association for Computational Linguistics (2007)
12. Kumar, S., Byrne, W.: Minimum bayes-risk decoding for statistical machine translation. Tech. rep., DTIC Document (2004)
13. Kumar, S., Macherey, W., Dyer, C., Och, F.: Efficient minimum error rate training and minimum bayes-risk decoding for translation hypergraphs and lattices. In: Proceedings of the Joint Conference of the 47th Annual Meeting of the ACL and the 4th International Joint Conference on Natural Language Processing of the AFNLP, vol. 1, pp. 163–171. Association for Computational Linguistics (2009)

14. Lafferty, J., McCallum, A., Pereira, F.C.: Conditional random fields: Probabilistic models for segmenting and labeling sequence data (2001)
15. Li, M., Duan, N., Zhang, D., Li, C.H., Zhou, M.: Collaborative decoding: Partial hypothesis re-ranking using translation consensus between decoders. In: Proceedings of the Joint Conference of the 47th Annual Meeting of the ACL and the 4th International Joint Conference on Natural Language Processing of the AFNLP, vol. 2, pp. 585–592. Association for Computational Linguistics (2009)
16. Och, F.J.: Minimum error rate training in statistical machine translation. In: Proceedings of the 41st Annual Meeting on Association for Computational Linguistics, vol. 1, pp. 160–167. Association for Computational Linguistics (2003)
17. Och, F.J., Ney, H.: A systematic comparison of various statistical alignment models. Computational Linguistics 29(1), 19–51 (2003)
18. Och, F.J., Ney, H.: The alignment template approach to statistical machine translation. Computational Linguistics 30(4), 417–449 (2004)
19. Papineni, K., Roukos, S., Ward, T., Zhu, W.J.: BLEU: a method for automatic evaluation of machine translation. In: Proceedings of the 40th Annual Meeting on Association for Computational Linguistics, pp. 311–318. Association for Computational Linguistics (2002)
20. Rosti, A.V.I., Ayan, N.F., Xiang, B., Matsoukas, S., Schwartz, R.M., Dorr, B.J.: Combining outputs from multiple machine translation systems. In: HLT-NAACL, pp. 228–235 (2007)
21. Sokolov, A., Wisniewski, G., Yvon, F.: Computing lattice BLEU oracle scores for machine translation. In: Proceedings of the 13th Conference of the European Chapter of the Association for Computational Linguistics, pp. 120–129. Association for Computational Linguistics (2012)
22. Stolcke, A., et al.: SRILM-an extensible language modeling toolkit. In: INTERSPEECH (2002)
23. Tian, L., Wong, D., Chao, L., Quaresma, P., Oliveira, F., Lu, Y., Li, S., Wang, Y., Wang, L.: UM-corpus: a large english-chinese parallel corpus for statistical machine translation. In: Proceedings of the 9th International Conference on Language Resources and Evaluation (2014)
24. Tromble, R.W., Kumar, S., Och, F., Macherey, W.: Lattice minimum bayes-risk decoding for statistical machine translation. In: Proceedings of the Conference on Empirical Methods in Natural Language Processing, pp. 620–629. Association for Computational Linguistics (2008)
25. Turchi, M., De Bie, T., Goutte, C., Cristianini, N.: Learning to translate: a statistical and computational analysis. In: Advances in Artificial Intelligence 2012, vol. 1 (2012)
26. Ueffing, N., Haffari, G., Sarkar, A.: Transductive learning for statistical machine translation (2007)
27. Wang, L., Wong, D.F., Chao, L.S., Xing, J.: CRFs-based chinese word segmentation for micro-blog with small-scale data. In: Proceedings of the Second CIPS-SIGHAN Joint Conference on Chinese Language, pp. 51–57. Citeseer (2012)
28. Wisniewski, G., Allauzen, A., Yvon, F.: Assessing phrase-based translation models with oracle decoding. In: Proceedings of the 2010 Conference on Empirical Methods in Natural Language Processing, pp. 933–943. Association for Computational Linguistics (2010)

Recognizing and Reordering the Translation Units in a Long NP for Chinese-English Patent Machine Translation

Xiaodie Liu[*], Yun Zhu, and Yaohong Jin

Institute of Chinese Information Processing, Beijing Normal University, Beijing, China
liuxiaodie2009@hotmail.com, zhuyun@bnu.edu.com,
jinyaohong@bnu.edu.cn

Abstract. This paper describes a rule based method to identify and reorder the translation units (a smallest unit for reordering) within a long Chinese NP for Chinese-English patent machine translation. By comparing the orders of translation units within long Chinese and English NPs, we developed a strategy on how to reorder the translation units according with the expression of English habit. By analyzing the features of translation units within a long Chinese NP, we built some formalized rules to recognize the boundaries of translation units using the boundary words to identify what to reorder. At last, we used a rule-based MT system to test our work, and the experimental results showed that our rule-based method and strategy were very efficient.

Keywords: reordering; rules-based, machine translation, patent.

1   Introduction

As a move to meet the global demand for Chinese patent information, Chinese-English machine translation in patent documents is becoming a hotspot in machine translation field. Machine translation (MT) has seen many exciting developments over the past decade, however, because the use of the language has the characteristics of obvious hierarchy: the sentence-groups level, the sentence level and the chunk[1] level [1], phrase-based models, syntax-based models, and dependency-based models cannot deal with the reordering at the sentence level very well, particularly the reordering in a hierarchical structure in which the inner reordering of Chinese NPs is dependent on.

The Hierarchical Semantic-Category-Tree (HSCT) model [1] used semantic features to handle the reordering at sentence level with a rule-based method. The system based on HSCT model could partition a sentence into chunks such as a predicate, subjects and objects wherein both can be long noun phases (NPs for short) etc. and reorder them in sentence level, but this system did not reorder the inner orders of translation units in a long NP. This paper aims to solve a type of the problem: recognizing and reordering the translation units in a long NP for Chinese-English Patent Machine Translation.

---

[*] Corresponding author.
[1] The chunks are directly constituent of a sentence, including predicates, subjects and objects.

X. Shi and Y. Chen (Eds.): CWMT 2014, CCIS 493, pp. 33–48, 2014.
© Springer-Verlag Berlin Heidelberg 2014

Especially, the language for patent usually was inclined to express complicated thought in long words. Here is an example wherein the number of the translation units in a long Chinese NP happens to be four.

Example:
Chinese NP: 一种TD_SCDMA系统中上行多小区联合检测的方法
English in Chinese order: a in a TD_SCDMA system uplink multi-cell joint detection method
Reference: a method of uplink multi-cell joint detection in a TD_SCDMA system
Result of Google: One kind TD_SCDMA system uplink multi-cell joint detection method.

According to the long Chinese NP and reference, there were four translation units in the long Chinese NP "一种在TD_SCDMA系统中上行多小区联合检测的方法": A"一种(a)", B"在TD_SCDMA系统中 (in a TD_SCDMA system)" , C "上行多小区联合检测(uplink multi-cell joint detection)"and D "方法(method)". The order of translation units in the Chinese NP was "A B C D" and the right English order of translation units was "A D C B" according to the reference.

However, according to the result of Google, the boundaries of "A, B, C and D" were unclear and the order of "A, B, C and D" in English was wrong.

How to recognize the boundaries of the translations such as two, three, four, five or more sub-NPs" and how to reorder them were the main problems that to be solved in this paper.

The remainder of this paper is organized as follows. In Section 2, we at first analyzed differences in the orders of long Chinese-English NPs and summed a strategy on how to reorder the translation units when translate the long Chinese NPs to English, then examined the features of translation units and sum boundary words for recognizing them. In Section 3, we used a rule-based method and designed an algorithm to recognize the translation units to solve what to reorder and how to reorder. In Section 4, we discussed the experiment results. Section 5 is the related work. Finally, a conclusion is given and the further work is expected in Section 6.

2   Analyses of the Chinese NPs

Based on aligned Chinese-English NPs from 15 Patent documents, we found the proportion of four types of Chinese NPs, whose units is two, three, four, five and more in table 1. It's important to note that the translation units were obtained by comparing the Chinese-English NPs, and the neighboring translation units were continuous string in the language.

Table 1. Distribution of Chinese NPs with Translation Units

Number of the units	2	3	4	5 and more
proportion	54%	29%	11%	6%

In this section, at first, we need define the translation unit based on comparing ample examples from Chinese-English languages. Second, we intent to develop a strategy on reorder Chinese NP based on analyzing the relations of translation units. Third, we explored how to identify the translation units to ensure our strategy could be realized.

2.1   Translation Units

Translation unit was defined in the perspective of Chinese with reference to the inner order of the long Chinese-English NPs translation. In a long NP, a translation unit was a word or word-group expressing the same meaning both in Chinese and English. Translation units were the equivalent in Chinese and English NPs, and it is certain that this study can only be based on contrasting the inner order of the long Chinese and English NPs. The long Chinese NP consists of sub-NPs or prepositional phrases (PP for short), locative phrase (LP for short) etc. The translation units were defined in perspective of Chinese only:

Sub-NP. Sub-NP was a smallest NP for reordering in Chinese-English machine translation It could be one or more word, such as "/详视图/(a detailed view) which is one word, /所述/局部/缩放/估算/器/(the said local scale estimator)" which is a sequence of five words 大部分常规的交通工具布线系统(most conventional vehicle wiring systems)" which could include a "的(de)" . The sub-NPs correspond to the English sub-NPs.

LP. LP consists of a sub-NP and a localizer, such as "燃料供给流路内(in a fuel supply passage) consisting of a sub-NP "燃料供给流路(a fuel supply passage)" and a localizer "内(in)"in the long NP "燃料供给流路内的气体压力(a gas pressure in a fuel supply passage)";

PP. There were three kinds, according to the constituents "sub-NP, preposition, localizer and structural word , etc".

PP consisting of a preposition and a sub-NP, such as "如权利要求1 (according to claim 1)" consisting of a preposition "如(according to)" and a sub-NP "权利要求1(claim 1)" in the long NP "如权利要求1所述的模具(a mould according to claim 1)" ;

PP consisting of a preposition, a sub-NP and a localizer, such as "在层流干燥炉中 (in a laminar flow oven)" consisting of a preposition "在(zai)", a sub-NP "层流干燥炉 (a laminar flow oven)"and a localizer "中(in)" in the long NP"在层流干燥炉中的过滤空气(filtered air in a laminar flow oven";

PP consisting of a preposition, some sub-NPs, a structural word and a localizer, such as "在本发明的实施例中" consisting of a preposition "在(zai)", two sub-NPs "本发明(the present invention) and 实施例(an embodiment)" ,a structural word "的(de)" and a localizer "中(in)"in long NP "在本发明的实施例中灌木丛移除器的立体图(an isometric view of a brush grubber in an embodiment of the present invention)";

The translation units should not be limited to the types described above, such as "塑料化合物等(such as a plastic compound) consisting of a sub-NPs "塑料化合物(a plastic compound)" ,a structural word "等(deng)" in long Chinese NP "塑料化合物等的复合树脂材料(a compound resin material such as a plastic compound)".

The Chinese NPs consist of sub-NPs, PPs, LPs and NP_Ns; otherwise, the English NPs consist of sub-NPs and PPs only.

2.2   How to Reorder the Translation Units

In Chinese-English MT, the structural difference in NPs between Chinese to English is a difficult problem, such as the different positions for the head of the NPs: the head of a Chinese NP is in the front; however that of an English NP is in the end. Therefore, the proper conversion of orders of the sub-NPs in long Chinese NPs into English also improves the naturalness and smoothness of the translated text. Once the translation units had been defined, a new strategy called reordering can be applied to them.

This part compared and analyzed the differences in the orders of Chinese-English NPs in patent so as to find out the language law and develop a strategy on how to translate the long Chinese NPs to English effectively.

According to the parallel Chinese-English NPs, we found that there are several types of translation units based on reordering:

- sub-NPs
- NP_Ns

   NP_Ns is unique to Chinese. It could be adjectives, pronouns, numerals and quantitative phrases in special position, such as "一些" which could occur in the NP "一些基于环保溶剂的清洗剂" which consist of three translation units "一些", "基于环保溶剂" and "清洗剂".

- PHs

   LP and PPs were collectively called PHs, because 1) they in Chinese correspond to the PPs English, and 2) they should be moved after sub-NPs when translating the Chinese into English.

The Chinese and English NPs share some characters in common: 1) the long NPs consist of PPs and sub-NPs, 2) the PPs could not be head of the long NP, 3) the NPs must be the head of the long NP.

However, the position and order between the sub-NPs and PPs in Chinese were different from English as the result of different culture and tradition, especially, the NP_Ns, LPs are unique for Chinese NPs. The primary dissimilarity is that the head translation unit must locate in the end and others translation units such as sub-NPs, PPs and LPs must be modifiers to some extent, otherwise, in English, the beginning translation unit is the head translation unit and followed by other PPs as modifiers.

Based on aligned Chinese-English NP-pairs from 15 Patent documents, this paper compared the differences in orders of Chinese-English NPs and analyzed types of translation units so as to find out the laws in translating Chinese NPs to English.

Long Chinese NPs with two translation units. All combinations and the structure relations about two translation units can be listed in table 2, and we can see that in combinations of "NP1 NP2", the NP1 or NP2 were the NPs and the NP1 must modify NP2; in combinations of "PH NP", the NP must be the NPs and PH must modify the NP.

For the PPs and LPs, the prepositions were before the NPs and the locatives were behind the NPs, but the PHs or LPs could be moved as a whole. In table 2, we can see that there only one reordering way for the Chinese NPs with two translation units and b).

Table 2. Orders of Chinese and English NPs with two translation units

	Order in Chinese		Order in English
	Combinations	Structure Relations	
a)	sub-NP1 sub-NP2[2]	([3]sub-NP1 sub-NP2)	sub-NP2 sub-NP1
b)	PH sub-NP	(PH sub-NP)	sub-NP PH

All structure relations between two translation units occur in Chinese, and we can find some examples to illustrate our reduction were right in table 3.

Table 3. Examples of orders of Chinese and English NPs with two translation units

Chinese Orders -> English orders
NP1 NP2-> NP2 NP1
(模制工艺)的(操作参数)->the operating parameters of the molding process
PH NP ->PH PP
(在前面实施方案中)(所述的相同类型的聚合材料)-> the same types of polymeric material in the earlier embodiment

Chinese NPs with three translation units. We can list all combinations and the structure relations about three translation units in the Chinese sub-NPs. In table 4, we can see that: a) has three structure relations: (sub-NP1 (sub-NP2 sub-NP3)) indicated that at first sub-NP2 modified sub-NP3, then they acted as a whole to be modified by sub-NP1, ((sub-NP1 sub-NP2) sub-NP3) indicated that at first sub-NP1 modified sub-NP2, then they acted as a whole to modify sub-NP3,and ((sub-NP1) (sub-NP2) sub-NP3) indicated that sub-NP1 and sub-NP2 respectively modify sub-NP3.b) has three structure relations: ((PH sub-NP1) sub-NP2) indicated that at first sub-NP1 modified sub-NP2, then they acted as a whole to be modified by PH, ((PH sub-NP1) sub-NP2) indicated that at first PH modified sub-NP1, then they acted as a whole to modify sub-NP2,and ((PH1)(sub-NP2) sub-NP3) indicated that PH and sub-NP1 respectively modify sub-NP2, and c) has three structure relations:(PH1 (PH2 sub-NP)) indicated that at first PH2 modified sub-NP, then they acted as a whole to be modified by PH1, ((PH1 PH2) sub-NP) indicated that PH1 and PH2 acted as a whole to modify sub-NP, and ((PH1)(PH2) sub-NP) indicated that PH1 and PH2 respectively modify sub-NP. d) has two structure relations: (sub-NP1 (PH sub-NP2)) indicated that at first PH modified sub-NP2, then they acted as a whole to be modified by sub-NP1, and ((sub-NP1)(PH)sub-NP2) indicated that sub-NP1 and PH respectively modify

---

[2]   The number behind NP or PH notes the order they appear in the linear sequence of Chinese NPs. The space among NP and PH is used to split the different translation units, and can stand for "的(de)" in authentic Chinese NPs.

[3]   Parentheses act as the relationships between modifier(the former) and head(the latter).

sub-NP2.e) has one structure relation (NP_N (PH sub-NP)) which indicated at first PH modified sub-NP, then they acted as a whole to be modified by NP_N.

Table 4. Orders of Chinese and English NPs with three translation units

	Order in Chinese Combinations"	Structure Relations	Order in English
a)	sub-NP1 sub-NP2 sub-NP3	(sub-NP1(sub-NP2 sub-NP3)) ((sub-NP1 sub-NP2) sub-NP3) ((sub-NP1)(sub-NP2) sub-NP3)	sub-NP3 sub-NP2 sub-NP1
b)	PH sub-NP1 sub-NP2	(PH (sub-NP1 sub-NP2)) ((PH sub-NP1) sub-NP2) ((PH)(sub-NP1) sub-NP2)	sub-NP2 sub-NP1 PH
c)	PH1 PH2 sub-NP	(PH1 (PH2 sub-NP)) ((PH1)(PH2) sub-NP) ((PH1 PH2) sub-NP)	sub-NP PH2 PH1 sub-NP PH1 PH2
d)	sub-NP1 PH sub-NP2	(sub-NP1 (PH sub-NP2)) ((sub-NP1)(PH)sub-NP2)	sub-NP2 PH sub-NP1
e)	NP_N PH sub-NP	(sub-NP_N (PH sub-NP))	NP_N sub-NP PH

Although, not all the structure relations among three translation units occur in Chinese, we can find some examples to illustrate our reduction were right in table 5.

Table 5. Examples of orders of Chinese and English NPs with three translation units

Chinese Orders -> English Orders
1 sub-NP1 sub-NP2 sub-NP3 -> sub-NP3   sub-NP2   sub-NP1 1.1((材料)的(捏合度))的(调节范围)->the adjusting range for the kneading degree of the material =>(sub-NP1 sub-NP2) sub-NP3 -> sub-NP3   sub-NP2   sub-NP1 1.2(这些模具)的((一种形式)的(结构))-> the construction of one form of the moulds =>sub-NP1 (sub-NP2 sub-NP3) -> sub-NP3   sub-NP2   sub-NP1
2 PH1 PH2 sub-NP-> sub-NP   PH2   PH1 (闸板部件接近于圆筒段时)的(材料间)的(捏合度)->the kneading degree between the material when the gate member is moved close to the cylindrical segment =>PH1 PH2 sub-NP-> sub-NP1   PH2   PH1

Table 5. (*Continued*)

3 PH sub-NP1 sub-NP2-> sub-NP2   sub-NP1   PH 3.1 ((在内模具部件上)的(第一密封装置))的(优点)-> the high vapor pressure of the propellant in the MDI =>(PH sub-NP1) sub-NP2-> sub-NP2   sub-NP1   PH 3.2 (调节捏合度时)的((装置)的(操作性))->the operability of the apparatus at the time of adjusting the kneading degree =>PH (sub-NP1 sub-NP2)-> sub-NP2   sub-NP1   PH
4 sub-NP1 PH sub-NP2-> sub-NP2 sub-NP1 PH (上述旋转轴部)的((绕水平轴)的(旋转力))-> the rotation force around the horizontal axis of the rotation axis part =>sub-NP1 PH+ +sub-NP2-> sub-NP2 sub-NP1 PH
5 NP_N PH   sub-NP-> NP_N   sub-NP   PH (一些）((基于环保溶剂)的(清洗剂))-> some cleaner based on environment-friendly   solvent =>NP_N PH sub-NP-> NP_N   sub-NP   PH

We all know that ambiguity can be caused by multiple and different semantic relations among translation units. So, how to reorder the three translation units seems to be a big problem. However we could conclude some laws about how to reorder the English orders of Chinese sub-NPs with three translation units as follows:

1) The reversed order is the only way for Chinese NPs "sub-NP1 sub-NP2 sub-NP3" which could have three modifications and three semantic relations;

2) The first sub-NP and the reversed order for PH is the only way for Chinese sub-NPs "PH PH sub-NP". For the pattern "((PH1 PH2) sub-NP)->sub-NP PH1 PH2", it only occurs in a kind of special Chinese sub-NPs, such as "从(from)......", "到/向 (to)......";

3) The first sub-NP2, second sub-NP1 and third PH is the only way for Chinese sub-NPs "PH sub-NP1 sub-NP2" which had three structure relations and for Chinese sub-NPs "sub-NP1 PH sub-NP2". For the pattern is (sub-NP1 PH sub-NP2)->sub-NP2 PH sub-NP1, the PH in English has the front boundary, and there is ambiguity, too;

4) The first NP_N, second sub-NP and third PH is the only way for long Chinese NPs "NP_N PH sub-NP" in e).

Synthesizing the above analytical results about the reordering of the long Chinese NP with two or three translation units, we design a strategy how to reorder the translation units:

Step1: recognizing the NP_N, PH sub-NP;

Step2: if there were NP_Ns, keeping the NP_Ns not moving and move the rest translation units in reverse;

Step3: moving all the PHs after the last sub-NPs,;

Step4:delete the "的(de)" and add the English word "of".

In theory, for the combination of Chinese NPs with four, five and more translation units may have many structures of modifications, but we can translate Chinese NPs to English NPs according to the strategy, which is a hypothesis.

2.3   How to Recognize the Translation Units

This part focused on examining the boundaries of translation units in long Chinese NP and tried to sum some semantic features of the boundaries and explore which words could function as boundaries to partition the Chinese NP into translation units.We sum outer Characteristics and inner Characteristics.

Outer Characteristics. In English, prepositions with flexible meanings are frequently used. They function as bonding agents in English NPs. In English NPs, the translation units can be obtained by the prepositions, such as "the spectral sensitivities of the image sensor device in red, blue, and green color channels", the prepositions "of" and "in" can partition the NP into three translation units: two sub-NPs "the spectral sensitivities", "the image sensor device", a PP "in red, blue, and green color channels". It's important to note, however, that the preposition "of" is especial in this paper and could divide a string into two adjacent translation units, for example the preposition "of" could divide a string "the spectral sensitivities of the image sensor device" into two adjacent translation units "the spectral sensitivities", " the image sensor device".

● structural particle "的(de)"

In Chinese NPs, the structural particle "的(de)" is similar to the preposition "of", but there is a difference between them.

Table 6. a simple comparison between preposition "of" and structural particle "的(de)"

	function	example
of	boundary	the opposed face 20 of the gate member 14 of the second embodiment
的 (de₁)	boundary	第2实施方式的闸板部件14的对置面20
的 (de₂)		一种独特的水性清洗成分(a unique water-based cleaning composition)

By comparing and analyzing the difference as well as locations between English modifiers and Chinese auxiliary words, the "的(de)" servers two functions in table 6. First, "的(de)", marked as "de₁", was a boundary of two translation units and should be excluded from the two translation units, such as the "的" in the long Chinese NP "第2 实施方式的闸板部件14的对置面20(the opposed face 20 of the gate member 14 of the second embodiment)", which consist three translation units "第2实施方式(the second embodiment)" ,"闸板部件14(the gate member 14)"and "对置面20(the opposed face 20)". second,"的(de)", marked as "de₂" , is an inner conjunction of a translation unit, such as the "的" in the NP "一种独特的水性清洗成分(a unique water-based cleaning composition)".

Here we focuses on "de$_1$" and should distinguish it from "de$_2$". Based on the studying of the "的(de)",we discovered some language rules from authentic contexts: "de$_2$" were often behind of words whose semantic features were property. In view of the simple processes, low cost and wide practicability, "de$_2$"can be eliminated more easily, when "的(de)" occurs behind the adjective, quantifier, verb, numeral phrase and pronoun etc. See some example of de$_2$ in table 7.

Table 7. Example of de$_2$

Context	Examples(Chinese->English)
Modal Verb+的	不必要的操作系数-> the unnecessary operating parameters
Pronoun+的	它们的历史功率-> their historical power
Adjective+的	有效的点击-> the effective electric shock
Numeral phrase+的	三个的防范装置-> three reflection preventing device
Verb +的	已涂覆的容器-> the coated container

From the above analysis we could see structural particle "的(de1)" could be outer boundaries words for recognize the translation units.

Inner Characteristics. In Chinese NPs, the sub-NPs may modify the sub-NPs with any explicit marks, such as prepositions, localizers and other auxiliary words, but they could not occur in English NPs. This section explores some laws at the beginning word and the end word of translation units in Chinese-English translation.

Chinese and English belong to two different language families, in most cases, the source language cannot correspond to the target language well. However, the internal components of translation units shared some characters in common as the result of linguistic universality and identity of human thinking form.

Left Characteristics. By comparing the translation units, we can obtain some features of the beginning of translation units, which can be some explicit and implicit boundaries of two translation units.
● prepositions

Preposition is one of Chinese functional words which have a complex function, involving various factors, such as "在(zai),根据(gen ju),作为(zuo wei)"etc.

● demonstrative pronoun
In English NPs, the translation units also can be obtained by the definite articles and demonstrative pronoun. In Chinese NPs, the translation units also can be obtained by demonstrative pronoun. For example, the word "这些(these)" is demonstrative pronoun in translation unit"这些业务(these services)".

● degree adverbs
The English adjective "notable" in translation unit "notable features" which are unique for English, thus appropriate version cannot find in Chinese vocabulary and expressed

in phases "很显著" in translation unit "很显著的特点", wherein "很" is a degree adverb. There are many degree adverbs in Chinese, for example "很(very),特别 (specially),极(too), 非常(extremely), 十分(very much),更(more), 较(better),比较 (better), 最(best)" etc.

● quantitative phrases

In Chinese NPs, the translation units could not obtained by indefinite articles and quantitative phrases. For example, the Chinese phases "一个(one),一种(one)" and so on correspond to the English words "a, an, one" .

The Chinese words "第一(first), 第二(second), 第三(third), 第四(forth)" correspond to the English words "first, second, third, fourth".

● adjectives

An adjective usually modifies the noun.

The difference of Chinese and English exists in many ways such as morphological structure and word-formation which leads to the different words for a semantic feature between Chinese and English. Some adjectives, past participles, present participles in English were expressed in phase in Chinese.

● negative adverbs

The English adjective negative prefixes, such as "negative, opposite, and reverse" etc, corresponds to the negative adverbial words "没有(dis-),不用 （un-）,不(un-),非(un-), 没(dis-),未 （dis-） "etc.

● time adverbs

The past participle "coated" in translation unit "coated tank" which are unique for English, thus appropriate version cannot find in Chinese vocabulary and expressed in phases "已涂覆" in translation unit "已涂覆罐", wherein "已" is a time adverb. There are many time adverbs in Chinese, for example "已经(already),曾经(once),早已(already),刚刚 (just now),正(be being),正在(be being),就(be going to),就要(be going to),将(be going to),将要(be going to),曾(once),刚(just now),才(already),在(be being)" etc.

● others

The "resulting" in translation unit "resulting decoded" which are unique for English, thus appropriate version cannot find in Chinese vocabulary and expressed in phases " 经解码" in translation unit "经解码语音".

The past participle "refrigerated" in translation unit "refrigerated substances" which are unique for English, thus appropriate version cannot find in Chinese vocabulary and expressed in phases "被制冷" in translation unit "被制冷物质", wherein "被" is an auxiliary word. There are many auxiliary words in Chinese, such as "所(suo)" etc.

The English adjective "movable" in translation unit "rotatable structure" which are unique for English, thus appropriate version cannot find in Chinese vocabulary and expressed in phases "可旋转" in translation unit "可旋转结构".

Right Characteristics By comparing the translation units, we can obtain some features of the end of translation units, which can be some explicit and implicit boundaries of two translation units.

- localizers

There is a special grammatical method in Chinese language—the words of locality which represent pure directions, such as "上(on),中(in),外(outside)".

- Noun

In general, the end of a translation unit in Chinese patent was a noun expressing the a person or an object etc.

- number words

The number words consist of the numbers from 0 to 9 and were labels related to the new inventions. Huge numbers of number words could not enter the knowledge base and were generated dynamically as NUM when knowledge base was loaded.

- letter words

The letter words consist of numbers from 0 to 9 and 26 English letters. As with the number words, Huge numbers of number words could not enter the knowledge base and were generated dynamically as SPN when knowledge base was loaded.

- other

The auxiliary word "等(Deng)" was used to display the enumeration entry. Some time nouns, such as "时(when)"and some auxiliary words, such as "而言(er yan)".

Table 8. The left boundary words and examples

Left Boundary Words	Examples
preposition	(一些)(基于环保溶剂)的(清洗剂)->(a number of)(cleaners)(based on environmentally friendly solvents)
demonstrative pronoun	(如权利要求5)(所述的方法)->(the method) (according to claim 5)
degree adverb	(这项发明)(非常显著地一个特点)->(a very significant feature) of (this invention)
quantitative phrase	(这种丙烯酸树脂)(一个来源)->(one suitable source) of (these acrylic acrylate resins)
adjective	(支撑表面)(可能的总体压力)->(the possible total fluid pressure)of(a support surface)
time adverb	(该容器)(已经清洗的表面)-> (the cleaned surface) of (the containers)
negative adverb	(取向膜) (未拉伸的酰化纤维素膜)-> (unstretched cellulose acylate films) of (Orientation film)
others	(该工件)(被照射区)-> (the irradiated region) of (the work)

As can be seen above, although Chinese does not have much overt morphology, it still distinguishes a translation unit from another by lexical devices. When they were not outer boundary words in one continuous string, we used demonstrative pronoun, degree adverb, time adverbs, quantitative phrase, adjective, negative adverbs and others as the left boundary words to partition the string into two translation units utilizing contextual clues such as right characteristics. See table 8 for examples. When they were not outer boundary words in one continuous string, we used number words, letter words, auxiliary word "等(Deng)" as the right boundary words to partition the string into two translation units.See table 9 for examples.

Table 9. The right boundary words and examples

Right Boundary Words	Examples
locative	(模具部件上)的(密封件)-> (a seal)(on the mould part)
number words	(水箱300)(底部组件303) ->(a base assembly 303)(for the tank 300)
letter words	(主体部400a)(膛)-> (the bore)of (the host section 400a)
等(deng)	(牵引电动机等) (负载装置)->(a load device)(such as the traction motor)

Some prepositions and some localizers work hand in hand, such as "在......中", " 当......时", "对......而言"etc.

The prepositions and localizers always worked with "de₁", for example, for Chinese NP "一种或多种作为湿润剂的醇类",the preposition "作为" and structural particle "de1" could partition it into three translation units, for Chinese NP "通常运转时的气体压力", the localizer "时"and structural particle "de1" could partition it into two translation units.

Taken together, the boundary words have two types: 1) The out boundary words ,such as "的(de)" ; 2) The inner boundary words, which include left boundary words and right boundary words. The left boundary words lie in the first word or phrase in a translation unit including propositions and the right boundary words lie in the last word including locatives.

3   Method

In our existing MT system, the Chinese NPs were given, but how to recognize the two or three translation units in the Chinese NPs were unknown. They can be obtained by using boundary words, for an effective boundary word or a combination of boundary words could not be the end or beginning of a base NP in semantic and partition a language string into two translation units.

3.1   Recognition

The boundary words have two types: 1) the out boundary word ,such as "的(de)" ;2) the inner boundary words, which include left boundary words and right boundary words. The left boundary words lie in the first word or phrase in a translation unit and the right boundary words lie in the last word.

The Chinese NPs are stored using a tree structure. Thus how to distinguish the "的 (de)" into "de$_1$" and "de$_2$", how to recognize the front and rear boundaries and how to combine the words of a unit is important.Using a rule-base method, we designed some tags and attributes for nodes to recognize the translation units:

Tags for Nodes. There were seven tags for tree nodes to partition the long Chinese NP into several translation units.

- MK
  MK was a node for "de$_1$" and means there is a reordering operation.
- MK_H
  MK_H need to add a new node "de$_1$" after the right boundary words.
- L1
  L1s were the front boundaries of translation units when the words were pre-positions.
- L1H
  L1Hs were the rear boundaries of translation units when the words were locatives.
- MK_Q
  MK_Q need to add a new node "de$_1$" before the left boundary words.
- GBK_B%
  GBK_B% was the beginning position of a long Chinese NP.
- GBK_E%
  GBK_E% was the end position of a long Chinese NP.

Attributes for Node. There were two attributes to indicate some operation for the nodes.

- LEVEL
  LEVEL was used to put on "的(de)",if value=-1, recognize it as "de$_1$", if value=0 (default value), recognize it as "de$_2$".
- NOT_CHANGE
  NOT_CHANGE was used to put on NP_N to keep it not moving.

We designed the algorithm as follows:

Step1: distinguishing the "的(de)" into "de$_1$" and "de$_2$"

- building 12 rules to rule out the "de2" by putting a value "2"to the attribute "level" of "的(de)" when the words before "的(de)" were adjective, quantifier, verb and pronoun;
- building 1 rule to identify the "de$_1$" by putting the "de$_1$" with a tag "MK";
  step2: recognizing the front and right boundaries
- recognizing the front boundaries L1 when the words were prepositions

- putting a tag "MK_Q" on the left boundary words when the words were nouns, NUM or SPN before the left boundary words (excluding prepositions);
- recognizing the rear boundaries L1H when the words were locatives etc;
- putting a tag "MK_H" on the right boundary words when the words behind the right boundary words were noun;

step3: Generating the PPs and NPs

- generating the PPs by combining the words   by the combination pattern[4] of boundary: (L1,L1H) (L1,L1] , [L1H,L1H), (L1,MK], [MK,L1], (GBK_B%,L1H), [MK,L1H) by programming.
- generating the NPs from some combinations of [L1H,GBK_E%), (MK,MK) by programming.
- generating the NP_Ns from some combinations of (GBK_B%,L1] by programming and put an attribute "NOT_CHANGE".

Through three steps above, we could obtain all the translation units "PPs, NPs and NP_Ns" for reordering.

3.2   Reordering

In reordering phase, we defined the head sub-NP at the end as NP_E. Then, the long NPs contained PHs, NP_Ns, DE1, sub-NP and NP_E. The strategies for reordering the Chinese NPs are as follows:

Step1: building 1 reorder rule for the Chinese NPs "NP_N PH sub-NP";

Step2: keeping the NP_Ns not moving and move the PPs behind the NP_Es in reverse;

Step3: moving the other sub-NPs behind the NP_Es in reverse,

Step4:delete the "的(de)" and add the English word "of".

4   Experiments and Results

In order to test the result of this rule-based method and the strategy of reordering, the experiments takes 500 authentic patent texts provide by SIPO as the training set. The evaluation will use the development data for the NTCIR-9 Patent Machine Translation Pilot Task, containing 2,000 bilingual Chinese-English sentence pairs. After integrating the method into an existing rule-based system (HSCTMT), we take a closed test on training set and an open text on evaluation set.

Table 10. Accuracy of Translation Units

System	Precision (%)
Closed test	95.34
Open test	90.17

---

[4]   Combination pattern (A,B) and [A,B] indicated combining the word from A to B, and "("indicate A or B was included, and A or B was excluded.

In table 10, the accuracy of translation units using boundary words in our system was very high and the results illustrated our rule-based method was efficient.

Table 11. Accuracy of Reordering of Chinese NPs in our system and Google

System	Closed test Precision (%)	Open test Precision (%)
HSCTMT	80.38	76.52
Google	53.27	55.95

In table 11, the result of two test shows the strategy of reordering was efficient, the semantic analysis in a rule-based method has effectively improved the recognition result of units for reordering, and Google performs poorly in tests.

There are two factors affecting the performance: 1) incorrect boundaries of the nested PPs and PPs with a boundary affected the results, such as the long NP "本发明的实施例中灌木丛移除器的立体图(an isometric view of a brush grubber in an embodiment of the present invention)" wherein we didn't clear whether the first "的" was in the domains of preposition "中" or not;2) the multi-category words affected the results.

5   Related Works

Many reordering methods or strategy have been proposed in recent years to address this problem from different aspects. Phrase-based models excel at capturing local reordering phenomena and memorizing multi-word translation [2], but they perform poorly in the long and nested sentences in Patent. Syntax-based models handle long-distance reordering better than phase-based models. Reference [3] introduced a set Syntax-based rules to decide if a DE construction should be reordered or not before translating to English. Reference [4] focused on a Chinese noun phrase [A DE B] and explored a log-linear DE classifier by using syntactic, semantic and discourse context to producing an English translation strategy. Reference [1] explored a Hierarchical Semantic-Category-Tree (HSCT) model, which present a sentence as a hierarchical structure based on the Hierarchical Network of Concepts theory(HNC theory) and handle the reordering in three levels: Sentence Level, Chunk Level and Word Level. Reference [5] designed a Chinese-English Patent Machine Translation system based on the HSCT model. Reference [6] designed a method to recognize the prepositional phrase. Reference [7,8] focused on reorder the inner components in some type NP of the long NP.

6   Conclusions and Future Work

Based on the analysis Chinese-English orders of Chinese NPs with two, three, four or more translation units, we developed a strategy on how to reorder the Chinese NPs. Based on analysis of translation units, we used a rule-based method to recognize the boundaries of the translation units using boundary words. The experimental results showed that our rule-based method and strategy were very efficient on the reordering the NPs.

In future, we will enrich and refine the rules to improve the performance and research on using statistical method to improve the translation performance.

Acknowledgement. The authors are grateful to Multi-level Knowledge Representation of Mass Texts and Chinese Language Understanding System (National 863 Program, No.2012AA011104) and the Fundamental Research Funds of Central Universities for financial support.

Reference

[1] Zhu, X., Jin, Y.: Hierarchical Semantic-Category-Tree Model for Chinese-English Machine Translation. China Communications, 80–92 (2010)

[2] Koehn, P., Marcu, D.: Statistical Phrase-based Translation. In: Proceeding of the 2003 Conference of the North American Chapter of the Association for Computational Linguistics on Human Language Technology, pp. 48–54 (2003)

[3] Wang, C., Collins, M., Koehn, P.: Chinese syntactic reordering for statistical machine translation. In: Proceeding of EMNLP-CoNLL, Prague, Czech Republic, pp. 737–745. Association for Computational Linguistics (June 2007)

[4] Chang, P., Jurafsky, D., Manning, C.D.: Disambiguating "DE" for Chinese-English Machine Translation. In: Proceeding fo the Fourth Workshop on Statistical Machine Translation, Athens, Greece, Association for Computational Linguistics, March 30-March 31, pp. 215–223. Association for Computational Linguistics (2009)

[5] Zhu, Y., Jin, Y.: A Chinese-English Patent Machine Translation System Based on the Theory of Hierarchical Network of Concepts. The Journal of China Universities and Tele-Communications, 140–146 (2012)

[6] Yin, L., Yao, T., Zhang, D., Li, F.: A Hybrid Approach of Chinese Syntactic and Semantic Analysis. China Information 04, 45–51 (2002) (in Chinese)

[7] Xiaodie, L., Yun, Z., Yaohong, J.: Research on Recognition of Chunks for Reordering in Chinese-English Patent Machine Translation. In: International Conference on Artificial Intelligence and Software Engineering, pp. 840–846 (2014)

[8] Xiaodie, L., Yun, Z., Yaohong, J.: Research on Reordering of the Chinese NPs A++B++C and Application. In: International Conference on Advances in Materials Science and Information Technologies in Industy, pp. 2253–2256 (2014)

A Statistical Method for Translating Chinese into Under-resourced Minority Languages

Lei Chen, Miao Li, Jian Zhang, Zede Zhu, and Zhenxin Yang

Institute of Intelligent Machines, Chinese Academy of Sciences
Hefei 230031, China
alan.cl@163.com, {mli,jzhang}@iim.ac.cn,
{zhuzede,xinzyang}@mail.ustc.edu.cn

Abstract. In order to improve the performance of statistical machine translation between Chinese and minority languages, most of which are under-resourced languages with different word order and rich morphology, the paper proposes a method which incorporates syntactic information of the source-side and morphological information of the target-side to simultaneously reduce the differences of word order and morphology. First, according to the word alignment and the phrase structure trees of source language, reordering rules are extracted automatically to adjust the word order at source side. And then based on Hidden Markov Model, a morphological segmentation method is adopted to obtain morphological information of the target language. In the experiments, we take the Chinese-Mongolian translation as an example. A morpheme-level statistical machine translation system, constructed based on the reordered source side and the segmented target side, achieves 2.1 BLEU points increment over the standard phrase-based system.

Keywords: Under-resourced languages, Mongolian, Reordering, Morphological segmentation, Machine translation.

1 Introduction

Compared with Chinese, most Chinese minority languages, such as Mongolian, Uyghur, etc., are under-resourced languages with different word order and rich morphology[2]. First, different from the subject-verb-object structures of Chinese, these minority languages are always in the subject-object-verb structures. Second, Chinese is an isolated language without any morphological changes. As highly agglutinative languages with a rich set of affixes, these minority languages may have a large quantities of word surface forms due to the inflectional and derivational productions. The incoordinate morphological information between Chinese and these under-resourced languages may cause serious data sparseness problem. Consequently, statistical machine translation (SMT) is difficult to achieve high performance in dealing with the translation between Chinese and these minority languages. According to the evaluation summary report of the 9th China Workshop on Machine Translation[17], the errors of the translation

X. Shi and Y. Chen (Eds.): CWMT 2014, CCIS 493, pp. 49–60, 2014.
© Springer-Verlag Berlin Heidelberg 2014

words choice and word order are two major errors of SMT systems. Therefore, how to reduce the differences of word order and morphology between Chinese and these minority languages is an important issue in SMT.

Taking Mongolian, one of Chinese minority languages, as an example, the paper proposes a method which incorporates syntactic information of the source-side and morphological information of the target-side. First, according to the word alignment and the phrase structure trees of source language, reordering rules are extracted automatically to adjust the word order at source side. And then at target side, a morphological segmentation method is adopted to obtain the morphological information of target language. The sentences consisting of Mongolian words are used to construct Hidden Markov Model (HMM) associated with the affixes. Based on this model, the affixes corresponding to the Mongolian words to be segmented are found to obtain the stems. This method transforms the segmentation problem into sequence labelling problem which is able to reduce the segmentation ambiguity. Taking advantage of the reordered source language and the segmented target language, a morpheme-level SMT system can be constructed. The experimental results show that the morpheme-level Chinese-Mongolian SMT system achieves 2.1 BLEU points increment over the standard phrase-based machine translation system.

2   Related Works

The reordering model is significant to improve the performance of translations. One kind of reordering models integrates the reordering knowledge into the log-linear statistical translation model as a feature, such as (Hou, *et al.*, 2009)[5], (Zhang and Zong, 2009)[25], (Feng, *et al.*, 2013)[4], etc. and more recent works (Li, *et al.*, 2014)[12], (Cao, *et al.*, 2014)[1], (Li, *et al.*, 2014)[13], etc. When languages pairs have the great differences of word order or morphology, this kind of reordering models may have difficulty in finding the required features. Meanwhile, the models will become more complicated and cost much more time after integrating the features in training and decoding. Another kind of reordering models uses a preprocessing to adjust the word orders of source language to be consistent with target language as much as possible, such as (Lee, *et al.* 2010)[11], (Visweswariah, *et al.*, 2010)[22], (Khalilov and Sima'an, 2011)[7], etc. The effect of this kind of reordering models depends on the reordering rules, which can be written artificially or extracted automatically from parallel corpus. (Liang, *et al.*, 2011)[15] and (Wangsiriguleng, *et al.*, 2011)[23] proposed some manually written reordering rules for the Chinese-Mongolian SMT. (Chen, *et al.*, 2013)[2] extracted rules automatically from a small-scale parallel corpus and made a comparison with the manually written rules in Chinese-Mongolian SMT. Of course, the two kinds of reordering models mentioned above are not exclusive for each other. Some models not only can be used as the preprocessing for source side reordering but also can be integrated into the decoder as a feature function, eg. (Yang, *et al.*, 2012)[24]. Since it is difficult to find the required features in the first kind of reordering models, and the manually written rules are inadequate to express the differences between Chinese and Mongolian, in this paper we take the second kind of reordering models which extracts rules automatically.

Morphological segmentation is another important way, which can reduce the morphological differences between isolated languages and agglutinative languages in SMT systems. Generally speaking, there are dictionary-based, rule-based and statistical methods for morphological segmentation. Dictionary-based methods construct the dictionaries of stems and affixes respectively and use match algorithm to match the words to be segmented with these dictionaries. Rule-based methods segment words according to the templates of some grammar rules. Statistical methods use the training data to learn and infer the possibility of language phenomena and composition. In practice, more than one method is used in combination at the same time. (Hou, *et al.*, 2009)[6] combined rule-based method and statistical method for segmenting Mongolian words. (Poon, *et al.*, 2009)[20] presented the first log-linear model, which used overlapping features and incorporated exponential priors inspired by the minimum description length principle, for unsupervised morphological segmentation of Arabic and Hebrew. The works of (Luong, *et al.*, 2010)[16] and (Wen Li, *et al.*, 2010)[14] indicated that applying morphological segmentation of morphologically rich languages is able to improve the translation quality of SMT systems. In this paper, we use the statistical methods for Mongolian morphological segmentation and combine the dictionary-based method to correct segmentation errors.

3   Reordering of the Source Language

3.1   Extraction of Reordering Rules

Most reordering methods are effective for local reordering in phrase-based SMT. However, as shown in Figure 1, word alignment indicates that long-distance reordering plays a key role in Chinese-Mongolian translation, which cannot be solved ideally at present.

Fig. 1. The word alignment of Chinese and Mongolian sentences

In this paper, we use the rules which imply the long-distance reordering information to adjust the word order of source language, namely Chinese. The effect of the manually written rules depends on the professional linguistic knowledge, which is considered as a drawback of this method. Hence, we investigate how to extract the reordering rules automatically based on the parallel corpus and word alignment.

The reordering rules are defined in the form of $N : x \rightarrow x'$, where N denotes a node in the phrase structure tree of source sentence, x denotes the child nodes of N in a left-to-right order which conform to the linguistic rules between language pairs, x' denotes the reordering sequence of x.

Given a source sentence s, the phrase structure tree of s is denoted by T_s. The set of the child nodes of a non-leaf node N is denoted by C_N. The average position of N corresponding to target side is calculated as follows:

$$avepos(N) = \frac{1}{C_N} \sum_{\omega \in C_N} pos(\omega) \qquad (1)$$

where $pos(\omega)$ is the position of the word ω corresponding to target side. After calculating the average position of each node in T_s, the reordered phrase structure tree, denoted by T_r, can be obtained. The reordering rules are extracted based on the set of tree pairs (T_s, T_r), which corresponds to all sentence pairs in the corpus. We choose the rules with the maximum probability $P(T_r|T_s)$, which is calculated as follows:

$$P(T_r|T_s) = \prod_{N \in I(T_s)} P(r(c_N)|c_N) \qquad (2)$$

where $I(T_s)$ denotes the set of internal nodes of T_s, c_N denotes the sequence of child nodes of the node N, and $r(c_N)$ denotes a reordering sequence of c_N. $P(r(c_N)|c_N)$ is calculated as follows:

$$P(r(c_N)|c_N) = \frac{count(r(c_N))}{count(c_N)} \qquad (3)$$

where $count(c_N)$ is the frequency of c_N occurrence in T_s and $count(r(c_N))$ is the frequency of $r(c_N)$ occurrence in T_r. Given a node N in T_s with k child nodes, there are $k!$ kinds of combinations of these nodes. The rules with the maximum probability are corresponding to the combinations with the maximum probability. Hence the reordering rules can be obtained. Table 1 gives some automatically extracted reordering rules from our parallel corpus.

Table 1. Some automatically extracted reordering rules

No.	Reordering rule
(1)	VP : VP$_1$ VP$_2$ → VP$_2$ VP$_1$
(2)	VP : VV PP → PP VV
(3)	VP : VV NP → NP VV
(4)	VP : VV QP → QP VV
(5)	VP : VV NP IP → IP NP VV
(6)	VP : DVP ADVP NP VP → ADVP NP DVP VP

3.2 Application of Reordering Rules

The reordering is carried out on the rule-matched subtrees of the phrase structure trees of source sentences. If a node n with its child nodes in phrase structure tree can match with the type of N and the x part of a rule r, then the child nodes of n are reordered according to the x' part of the rule r. After traversing all the nodes in phrase structure tree, the reordering is achieved. Figure 2 show the effect of applying some reordering rules, where Figure 2(a) gives a phrase structure tree of the example Chinese sentence in Figure 1 and Figure 2(b) gives the reordered result.

We can see that after reordering two verb phrases, the cross-connect lines corresponding to the word alignment are all reduced, which means that the order

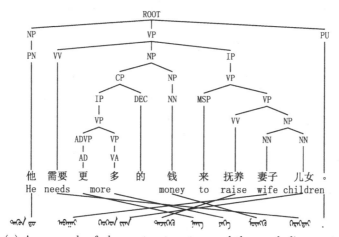

(a) An example of phrase structure tree and the word alignment

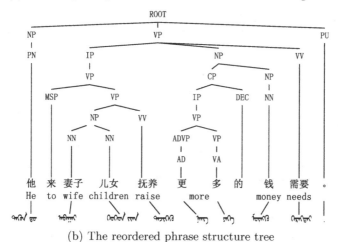

(b) The reordered phrase structure tree

Fig. 2. The application of reordering rules

of the example Chinese sentence is adjusted to be consistent with Mongolian. The example indicates that the application of the automatically extracted rules is effective.

4 Morphological Segmentation of the Target Language

4.1 HMM-Based Morphological Segmentation

Hidden Markov model is a quintuple $u = (\Omega, \Sigma, A, B, \Pi)$, where Ω is the state alphabet set, Σ is the observation alphabet set, A is the state transition array, B is the output probability array, storing the probability of observation, and Π is the initial probability array. In order to construct the Hidden Markov model associated with the Mongolian affixes, the sentences consisting of Mongolian words and the affixes sequence are considered as the observation sequence and the state sequence respectively. Therefore, the state alphabet set Ω, the observation alphabet set Σ and the initial probability array Π of affixes can be learned from the training corpus. The state transition array A is calculated as follows,

$$A = \{a_{ij} = P(X_{t+1} = S_j | X_t = S_i) = \frac{count(X_t = S_i, X_{t+1} = S_j)}{count(X_t = S_i)}\} \quad (4)$$

where $count(X_t = S_i, X_{t+1} = S_j)$ denotes the number of the current affix S_i to the next affix S_j and $count(X_t = S_i)$ denotes the number of the occurrences of the affix S_i. The output probability array B is calculated as follows,

$$B = \{b_{ik} = P(Y_t = O_k | X_t = S_i) = \frac{count(X_t = S_i, Y_t = O_k)}{count(X_t = S_i)}\} \quad (5)$$

where $count(X_t = S_i, Y_t = O_k)$ denotes the number of the observed word O_k with the affix S_i.

Given a Mongolian sentence consisting of the observation word sequence $O = O_1 O_2 ... O_T$, the segmentation problem is transformed into how to calculate the following state sequence which can optimally illustrate the observation. We use the Viterbi algorithm to solve the problem.

$$S^* = \arg\max P(S|O, u) \quad (6)$$

Example 1 gives an example of HMM-based morphological segmentation for Mongolian (in Latin form), where "Nosuf" denotes no affix.

Example 1. Transforming the word sequence into the word/affix sequence.

- Word sequence:
  TETE-BER HOTA-YIN TOB ORTEGEN-ECE TAKSI-DV SAGVBA .
- Word/affix sequence:
  TETE-BER/-BER HOTA-YIN/-YIN TOB/NoSuf ORTEGEN-ECE/NoSuf
  TAKSI-DV/LG_A+HV-DV SAGVBA/BA ./NoSuf

We can see that most segmentations in Example 1 are correct. However, unfortunately, segmentation errors still exist. The affix "LG_A+HV-DV" segmented from the word "TAKSI-DV" is wrong. Hence, we also study the method for segmentation error correction.

4.2   Segmentation Error Correction

The segmentation error correction includes the following two steps.

- First, finding the most likely word in the vocabulary list which is generated based on the vocabulary model of words and affixes.
- Otherwise, finding the maximum matching affix according to the affix string list which is generated based on the meta model of affixes by using the reverse maximum matching method.

The vocabulary model of words and affixes is defined by

$$M =< w, [< a_1, c_1 >, < a_2, c_2 >, ...] >,$$

where w is a word, a_i denotes the possible affix corresponding to w, and c_i denotes the number of occurrences of a_i. The vocabulary list generated based on this model is defined by

$$V = \{w_i, [< a_{i1}, c_{i1} >, < a_{i2}, c_{i2} >, ...]\}.$$

Given a word w_i with the wrong affix a_i, the concrete procedure of segmentation error correction is given as follows.

(1) If the word w_i is found in the vocabulary list, correcting the corresponding affix $a_i = \{a_{ij}|c_{ij} \geq max(c_{ik}), < a_{ij}, c_{ij} >, j \neq k\}$.
(2) Otherwise, reversely searching w_i to find the affixes satisfied the affix string list, denoted by $A_{al} = \{a_k|c_k = F(a_k) \vee G(a_k), a_k \in A_l\}$, where c_k is the reverse found string, A_l is the affix string list (shown in Example 2), a_k is the affix string, $F(a_k)$ is the affix string which removes the symbol "+" from a_k, and $G(a_k)$ is the affix string which removes the symbols "+" and "_" from a_k.
(3) Calculating the maximum affix from all the found affixes to correct a_i as follows, $a_i = \{a_k|L(F(a_k)) \geq max(L(F(a_j))), a_j \in A_{al}, a_k \in A_{al}, j \neq k\}$, where $L(F(a_k))$ is the length of $F(a_k)$.
(4) Finding the most likely affix in the vocabulary list to correct the possible wrong affix "NoSuf".

Example 2. An affix string list generated based on the meta model of affixes.

+CI+GSAN

+GCI-ECE

+G_A+GDA+GSAN-IYAR

+JAG_A

-TEGEN

. . .

According to the above method, some wrong affixes predicted by HMM can be corrected. Example 3 gives the correction of Example 1, where "N-ECE" and "-DV" are the correct affixes.

Example 3. Segmentation error correction of Example 1.

– Word sequence:
  TETE-BER HOTA-YIN TOB ORTEGEN-ECE TAKSI-DV SAGVBA .
– Wrong word/affix sequence:
  TETE-BER/-BER HOTA-YIN/-YIN TOB/NoSuf ORTEGEN-ECE/NoSuf
  TAKSI-DV/LG_A+HV-DV SAGVBA/BA ./NoSuf
– Revised word/affix sequence:
  TETE-BER/-BER HOTA-YIN/-YIN TOB/NoSuf ORTEGEN-ECE/N-ECE
  TAKSI-DV/-DV SAGVBA/BA ./NoSuf

5 Experiments

5.1 Reordering

The experimental platform of reordering is built based on the open source decoder Moses[9]. The Chinese sentences are parsed by the toolkit Stanford parser[8] in order to obtain the phrase structure trees. The default grow-diag-final heuristic[10] is used in GIZA++ to obtain the bidirectional word alignments. All 3-gram language models with Kneser-Ney smoothing are built by the SRI language modeling toolkit[21]. The log-linear model feature weights are learned by using minimum error rate training[18] with BLEU score[19] as the objective function. As the training set, the small parallel corpus contains 67288 Chinese-Mongolian sentence pairs, which is obtained from the 5th China Workshop on Machine Translation (CWMT 2009). The traditional Mongolian has been converted into Latin form before the model training. The test set and development set contain 400 sentences respectively, where each sentence has four reference translations.

Even though the parallel corpus is very small, compared with some other corpus with millions of sentence pairs, we found that too many reordering rules may be extracted automatically . Actually, there are more than one thousand reordering rules extracted automatically from the small Chinese-Mongolian parallel corpus, which may cause the conflict of rule-choosing or over-reordering frequently. Therefore, the probability of each rule is defined to alleviate the problem. Besides, adding some grammatical restrictions can play a similar role. For instance, the alignment results obtained by GIZA++ with grow-diag-final heuristic can be used to restrict some possible over-reordering. That is, if a node with its child nodes of the phrase structure tree matches with a reordering rule, the child nodes are reordered only if the average position of all leaf nodes of the leftmost branch is greater than the one of any right branch. Note that if a leaf node is not aligned with the target side, the leaf node will be ignored when the average position is calculated.

The experimental results of reordering are shown in Table 2, where "PB" denotes the result of the standard phrase-based system, "HPB" denotes the result of the hierarchical phrase-based system and "Reordering" denotes the

Table 2. The experimental results of reordering

System	BLEU score (%)	NIST score
PB	22.74	5.5466
HPB	23.24	5.5761
Reordering	23.85	5.6141

result of applying the automatically extracted rules. Both BLEU score and NIST score[3] are included to evaluate the results.

The experimental results show that the BLEU score of the Reordering system achieves 1.11 percent increment over the standard phrase-based system and 0.61 percent increment over the HPB system, which indicates that the application of the automatically extracted reordering rules can improve the SMT performance evidently.

5.2   Morphological Segmentation

In the experiments, the test parallel corpus contains 38000 Chinese-Mongolian sentence pairs, together with 330,000 Mongolian words, which are segmented to stems and affixes manually. We conduct three groups of experiments. In each group, 500 sentences are randomly extracted as the test set and the 37500 sentences left are the training set. We use the measure *Precision* to evaluate the results of morphological segmentation, calculated by $Precision = N_c/N$, where N_c is the number of correct segmentation and N is the total number of segmentation. Table 3 gives the results, where "$Precision_1$" is the result of original HMM-based morphological segmentation and "$Precision_2$" is the result of applying segmentation error correction on each group.

Table 3. The experimental results of morphological segmentation

Group	$Precision_1$ (%)	$Precision_2$ (%)
(1)	92.2574	96.4573
(2)	92.2403	95.6481
(3)	92.2212	96.6078
Average	92.2396	96.2377

The experimental results show that the HMM-based morphological segmentation, especially after applying segmentation errors correction, is effective, achieving the 96.2377% score when the vocabulary model, the meta model of affixes and the reverse maximum matching method are adopted.

5.3   Morpheme-Level SMT

In this experiment, the reordered Chinese sentences and the segmented Mongolian sentences are considered as the new parallel corpus to construct the morpheme-level SMT system. Hence, each word of translations consists of a stem and some affixes, which can be expressed by the following regular expression: $Word=Stem+ (+Suf)*$, where the symbol "+" is used to restore stems to surface words after decoding. Example 4 gives an original Mongolian sentence and the corresponding form in the morpheme-level corpus.

Example 4. An original Mongolian sentence and its morpheme-level form:

- The original sentence:
  TEGUN-U JOBLELGE-YI ESE HULIYEN ABVBAL HARAMSA
- The morpheme-level form:
  TEGUN+ +-U JOBLELGE+ +-YI ESE+ HULIYE+ +N ABV+ +BAL HARAMSAL+

The experimental setup is similar to the reordering experiments. Since each Mongolian word can be segmented into 1.5 morphemes on average, the lengths of morphemes are shorter than words. Besides the "PB" system and the "Reordering" system, we conduct another four groups of experiments, where the main changes are language model and maximum phrase length. Table 4 gives the evaluation of each morpheme-level SMT system, where "LM" denotes language model, "MPL" denotes maximum phrase length.

Table 4. Evaluation of the morpheme-level SMT system

System	LM	MPL	BLEU score (%)	NIST score
PB	3-gram	7	22.74	5.5466
Reordering	3-gram	7	23.85	5.6141
Morpheme-level$_1$	3-gram	7	24.26	5.6676
Morpheme-level$_2$	3-gram	10	24.52	5.6833
Morpheme-level$_3$	4-gram	7	24.61	5.7265
Morpheme-level$_4$	4-gram	10	24.84	5.7128

From Table 4, we can see that the highest BLEU score is 24.84%, which achieves 2.1 points increment over the "PB" system. The probabilities of morphemes are increased when the Mongolian words are segmented into stems and affixes, which can improve the performance of the Chinese-Mongolian SMT system. However, complete segmentation bring about some morpheme missing in decoding such that these morphemes can not be restored in postprocessing, which causes the evaluation improving not obvious sometimes.

6   Concluding Remarks

The paper proposed a statistical method for translating Chinese into under-resourced minority languages. The method incorporates syntactic information of source-side and morphological information of target-side to reduce the differences of word order and morphology in SMT system. Taking advantage of the reordered source language and the segmented target language, a morpheme-level SMT system can be constructed. We conducted some experiments to validate this method in Chinese-Mongolian SMT, where the BLEU score achieved 2.1 points increment over the standard phrase-based SMT system. Although only Mongolian is taken as an example in this paper, the method is still available for other under-resourced minority languages.

Future work includes: improving the precisions of syntax parsing and word alignment, which are significant in extracting reordering rules; alleviating the conflict of reordering rules by integrating some language knowledge; verifying the method for more under-resourced minority languages.

Acknowledgments. The authors would like to thank the anonymous reviewers for their helpful reviews. The work is supported by the Informationization Special Projects of Chinese Academy of Science under No. XXH12504-1-10.

References

1. Cao, H., Zhang, D., Li, M., Zhou, M., Zhao, T.: A Lexicalized Reordering Model for Hierarchical Phrase-based Translation. In: COLING, pp. 1144–1153 (2014)
2. Chen, L., Li, M., Zhang, J., Zeng, W.: Reordering for Chinese-Mongolian SMT Based on Small Parallel Corpus. Journal of Chinese Information Processing 27(5), 198–204 (2013) (in Chinese)
3. Doddington, G.R.: Automatic Evaluation of Machine Translation Quality Using N-gram Co-Occurrence Statistics. In: HLT, pp. 138–145 (2002)
4. Feng, M., Peter, J.T., Ney, H.: Advancements in Reordering Models for Statistical Machine Translation. In: ACL, pp. 322–332 (2013)
5. Hou, H., Liu, Q., Li, J.: A Phrase-based Statistical Chinese-Mongolian Machine Translation and Reordering Model. Chinese High Technology Letters 19(5), 475–479 (2009) (in Chinese)
6. Hou, H., Liu, Q., Nasanurtu, Murengaowa, Li, J.: Mongolian Word Segmentation Based on Statistical Language Model. Pattem Recognition and Aitificial Intelligence 22(1), 108–112 (2009) (in Chinese)
7. Khalilov, M., Sima'an, K.: Context-Sensitive Syntactic Source-Reordering by Statistical Transduction. In: IJCNLP, pp. 38–46 (2011)
8. Klein, D., Manning, C.D.: Accurate unlexicalized parsing. In: ACL, pp. 423–430 (2003)
9. Koehn, P., Hoang, H., Birch, A., Callison-Burch, C., Federico, M., Bertoldi, N., Cowan, B., Shen, W., Moran, C., Zens, R., Dyer, C., Bojar, O., Constantin, A., Herbst, E.: Moses: Open Source Toolkit for Statistical Machine Translation. In: ACL, pp. 177–180 (2007)
10. Koehn, P., Och, F.J., Marcu, D.: Statistical Phrase-Based Translation. In: HLT-NAACL, pp. 48–54 (2003)
11. Lee, Y.S., Zhao, B., Luo, X.: Constituent Reordering and Syntax Models for English-to-Japanese Statistical Machine Translation. In: COLING, pp. 626–634 (2010)
12. Li, J., Marton, Y., Resnik, P., Daume III, H.: A Unified Model for Soft Linguistic Reordering Constraints in Statistical Machine Translation. In: ACL, pp. 1123–1133 (2014)

13. Li, P., Liu, Y., Sun, M., Izuha, T., Zhang, D.: A Neural Reordering Model for Phrase-based Translation. In: COLING, pp. 1897–1907 (2014)
14. Li, W., Chen, L., Wudabala, Li, M.: Chained Machine Translation Using Morphemes as Pivot Language. In: Workshop on Asian Language Resouces at COLING, pp. 169–177 (2010)
15. Liang, F., Chen, L., Li, M., Nasun-urtu: A Rule-based Source-side Reordering on Phrase Structure Subtrees. In: IALP, pp. 173–176 (2011)
16. Luong, M.T., Nakov, P., Kan, M.Y.: A Hybrid Morpheme-Word Representation for Machine Translation of Morphologically Rich Languages. In: EMNLP, pp. 148–157 (2010)
17. Lv, Y.: Evaluation Summary of the 9th China Workshop on Machine Translation. In: CWMT (2013), `http://www.liip.cn/cwmt2013/evaluation.html`
18. Och, F.J.: Minimum Error Rate Training in Statistical Machine Translation. In: ACL, pp. 160–167 (2003)
19. Papineni, K., Roukos, S., Ward, T., Zhu, W.J.: BLEU: a Method for Automatic Evaluation of Machine Translation. In: ACL, pp. 311–318 (2002)
20. Poon, H., Cherry, C., Toutanova, K.: Unsupervised Morphological Segmentation with Log-Linear Models. In: HLT-NAACL, pp. 209–217 (2009)
21. Stolcke, A.: SRILM - An Extensible Language Modeling Toolkit. In: Proc. Intl. Conf. on Spoken Language Processing, pp. 901–904 (2002)
22. Visweswariah, K., Navratil, J., Sorensen, J., Chenthamarakshan, V., Kambhatla, N.: Syntax Based Reordering with Automatically Derived Rules for Improved Statistical Machine Translation. In: COLING, pp. 1119–1127 (2010)
23. Wangsiriguleng, Siqintu, Nasan-urtu: A Reordering Method of Chinese-Mongolian Statistical Machine Translation. Journal of Chinese Information Processing 25(4), 88–92 (2011) (in Chinese)
24. Yang, N., Li, M., Zhang, D., Yu, N.: A Ranking-based Approach to Word Reordering for Statistical Machine Translation. In: ACL, pp. 912–920 (2012)
25. Zhang, J., Zong, C.: A Framework for Effectively Integrating Hard and Soft Syntactic Rules into Phrase Based Translation. In: PACLIC, pp. 579–588 (2009)

Character Tagging-Based Word Segmentation for Uyghur

Yating Yang[1], Chenggang Mi[1,2], Bo Ma[1], Rui Dong[1,2], Lei Wang[1], and Xiao Li[1]

[1] Xinjiang Technical Institute of Physics & Chemistry of Chinese Academy of Sciences,
Urumqi, Xinjiang 830011, China
[2] University of Chinese Academy of Sciences, Beijing, 100049, China
{yangyt,dongrui,wanglei,xiaoli}@ms.xjb.ac.cn,
michenggang@gmail.com, yanyushu_xj@sina.com

Abstract. For effectively obtain information in Uyghur words, we present a novel method based on character tagging for Uyghur word segmentation. In this paper, we suggest five labels for characters in a Uyghur word, include: Su, Bu, Iu, Eu and Au, according to our method, we segment Uyghur words as a sequence labeling procedure, which use Conditional Random Fields (CRFs) as the basic labeling model. Experimental show that our method collect more features in Uyghur words, therefore outperform several traditional used word segmentation models significantly.

Keywords: Word segmentation, Uyghur, Conditional Random Fields, Character Tagging.

1 Introduction

Statistical natural language processing [1] [2] is widely used in recent years, which focus on corpus-driven methods that make use of supervised and unsupervised machine learning approaches and algorithms [3]. However, in statistical natural language processing, data sparseness is always a problem, especially for languages like Uyghur.

Uyghur is a Turkic language with millions of speakers mainly in the Xinjiang Uyghur Autonomous Region in the north west of China, where it is one of official languages. The Xinjiang Uyghur is used in the media, and as a lingua franca among other people. There are also communities of Uyghur speakers in Kazakhstan and Uzbekistan. Like many other Turkic languages, Uyghur displays vowel harmony and agglutination, lacks noun classes or grammatical gender, and is left-branching language with subject-object-verb word order.

   1)   Examples of Uyghur word forming:

我的包(My bag): سومكا + م -) سومكام
suffix0   *stem*

您的书(Your book): كىتاب + ىڭىز -) كىتابىڭىز
suffix0   *stem*

X. Shi and Y. Chen (Eds.): CWMT 2014, CCIS 493, pp. 61–69, 2014.
© Springer-Verlag Berlin Heidelberg 2014

ئىشلە + م + سىز + «ئىشلەمسىز
suffix1 suffix0 stem

你工作了吗? (Do you have a job?):

2) Examples of word order in Uyghur:

ئىشلەيسىز؟ نەدە سىز
Verb   Object Subject

您在哪? (Where are you?)

مەن تاماق يىمەيمەن
Verb   Object Subject

我不吃饭。(I don't want to eat.)

Due to the rich morphology and low-resourced of Uyghur, data sparseness always occur when dealing with Uyghur information with statistical methods. For alleviate this problem, many word segmentation methods have been proposed. However, previous work toke a Uyghur word as the unit, which not utility features of Uyghur words sufficiently. In this paper, we present a Uyghur word segmentation model, which take a Uyghur characters basic unit, and consider the Uyghur word segmentation as a classification procedure. Experimental results show that, our model collect more features for the classifier, and outperform other mostly used segmentation methods.

2   Related Work

Many previous works focused on Uyghur word segmentation. Zaokere et.al suggested a Uyghur noun stemming system based on hybrid method, whichused Finite State Machine (FSM) to stem the Uyghur noun word, and disambiguated ambiguous suffixes with Maximum Entropy model [4].Zou et.al recognized Uyghur event-anchored temporal expressions used stemming method [5].Xue et.al presented an unsupervised Uyghur word segmentation method based on affix corpus, which segmented words by rules with affix corpus, scored word segmentations with MAP model, and selected the one with highest score as the right segmentation [6].Chen proposed a stem segmentation method, which combined the Bidirectional Matching algorithm and Omni-word Segmentation algorithm; the precision of the stem segmentation had been improved. Also, the improved binary-seek-by-character dictionary mechanism was employed in the application of Uyghur stem segmentation and it could improve the efficiency [7].For handled the basic phonetic features of Uyghur words, such as the final vowel change, rules of vowel and consonant harmony, and syllable segmentation. Gulila et al. summarized the word structures and phonetic structures of Uyghur, and proposed some rules of Uyghur word segmentation and implementation of this segmentation [8].

3   Conditional Random Fields Model

Conditional random fields (CRFs) [9] [10] [11] are a type of statistical modeling method often used in pattern recognition and machine learning, where they are used for structured prediction. Whereas an ordinary classifier predicts a label for a single sample without regard to "neighboring" samples, a CRF can take context into account. CRFs are also a class of discriminative undirected probabilistic graphical model. It is used to encode known relationships between observations and construct consistent interpretations. It is often used for labeling or parsing of sequential data, such as natural language text or biological sequences and in computer vision. Specifically, CRFs find applications in shallow parsing, named entity recognition and gene finding, among other tasks, being an alternative to the related hidden Markov models [12] [13].

3.1   Definition of CRF

A CRF on observation X and random variables Y is defined as follows:

Let $G = (V, E)$ be a graph such that $Y = (Y_v)_{v \in V}$, so that Y is indexed by the vertices of G. Then (X, Y) is a conditional random field when the random variables Y_v conditioned on X, obey the Markov property with respect to the graph: $p(Y_v \mid X, Y_w, w \neq v) = p(Y_v \mid X, Y_w, w \sim v)$, where $w \sim v$ means that w and v are neighbors in G. A CRF is an undirected graphical model whose nodes can be divided into exactly two disjoint sets X and Y, the observed and output variables, respectively; the conditional distribution $p(Y \mid X)$ is then modeled.

3.2   Using CRFs to Label Sequence

In sequence modeling, the graph of interest is usually a chain graph. An input sequence of observed variables X represents a sequence of observations and Y represents a hidden (or unknown) state variable that needs to be inferred given the observations.

The conditional dependency of each Y_i on X is defined through a fixed set of feature functions of the form $f(i, Y_{i-1}, Y_i, X)$, which can be informally be thought as measurements on the input sequence that partially determine the likelihood of each possible value for Y_i. The model assigns each feature a numerical weight and combines them to determine the probability of a certain value for Y_i.

3.3   Why Conditional Random Fields?

Because of following reasons, we choose CRFs as the classification model in our Uyghur words segmentation.
1)   Sound and understood principle (maximum entropy) [14] [15][16][17];
2)   Very flexible for feature definition;
3)   Natively handling sequences;
4)   State of the art results on numerous applications.

4   Character Tagging

In this part, we describe the tagging procedure of Uyghur words for word Segmentation.

4.1   Features of Uyghur

A Uyghur word can be formed as:

$$word = stem + suffix_1 + suffix_2 + \cdots + suffix_n \tag{1}$$

Here, stem is a Uyghur stem, $suffix_i$ is the ith suffix in a Uyghur word. N is the number of suffixes in a Uyghur word.

For example:

我的包(My bag) :   سومكا + م ‹- سومكام
                              suffix0   *stem*

您的书(Your book) :   كىتاب + ىڭىز ‹- كىتابىڭىز
                              suffix0   *stem*

你工作了吗? (Do you have a job?):   ئشله + م + سىز ‹- ئشلەمسىز
                                           suffix1 *suffix0* *stem*

Common used Uyghur word segmentation models took the stem and suffixes of a Uyghur word as entire parts, respectively, which ignored inner relationship among characters. In this paper, we consider the features of Uyghur and the data sparseness of language resource, labeling characters according to their positions in a Uyghur word, and then, we train a CRFs based sequence labeling model. Details of characters labeling are shown in next part.

4.2   Tagging

For fully obtain features between characters in a Uyghur word, or even in a short Uyghur text, we suggest five labels in our method, which include: Su, Bu, Iu, Eu and Au.

1) **Su** - A word include a single character
2) **Bu** – The start character of a Uyghur word stem
3) **Iu** – characters between the start character and the end character in a Uyghur word stem
4) **Eu** – The end character of a Uyghur word stem
5) **Au** – Characters in suffixes of a Uyghur word
6) **Space** – Spaces between words. According to our method, we only keep one space between Uyghur words. (Which completed in preprocessing part)

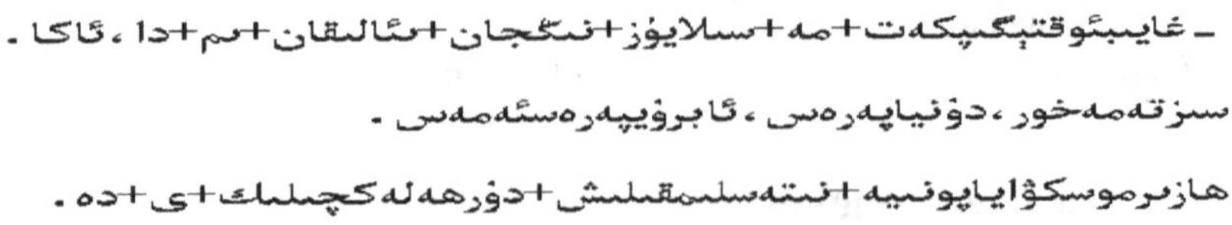

ـ غايىبئوقتىپگىپكەت+مە+سىلايىۇز+نىگجان+ئالىقان+مىم+دا، ئاكا .

سىزتەمەخور، دۇنيابەرەس، ئابرۇپپەرەستئەمەس .

هازىرموسكۇئايايىۇنىپە+ئىنتەسلىمقىلىش+دۇرھەلە كچىمللك+ى+ە .

Fig. 1. Three Uyghur sentences before tagging

Au/م Eu/ت Iu/ه Bu/ك Eu/پ Iu/ى Iu/ی Iu/گ Iu/ي Bu/ت Eu/ق Iu/و Bu/ئ Eu/ب Iu/ى Iu/ي Iu/ا Bu/غ
Iu/ا Bu/ئ Au/ى Eu/ن Iu/ا Bu/ج Au/ڭ Au/ى Au/ن Eu/ز Iu/ز Bu/ي Au/ا Au/ل Au/ى Au/س Au/ه
ه/Su Iu/ا Bu/ك Iu/ا Bu/ئ Su،Au/ ا Au/د Au/م Au/ى Eu/ن Iu/ا Iu/ق Iu/ى Iu/ل.

مس Bu/ى Iu/ى Eu/ز Eu/ت Bu/ه Iu/ه Iu/م Iu/خ Iu/و Iu/ ر Su،Eu/ د Bu/ؤ Iu/ن Iu/ي Iu/ا Iu/پ Iu/ى Iu/ر
ه Iu/ س Iu/م/Su،Eu/ئ Eu/س Bu/ئ Iu/ه Iu/م Iu/ه Iu/ر Iu/ؤ Iu/ي Iu/پ Iu/ب Iu/ا Bu/ئ
مس/Su.

هه Bu/ا Iu/ز Iu/ ی Iu/ى Eu/ر Bu/م Bu/و Iu/س Iu/ا Iu/ك ؤ Iu/ا Eu/ي Bu/ا Iu/ا Iu/پ Iu/و Iu/ن Iu/ ی Iu/ي Eu/ه
ن Au/ى Au/ت Bu/ه Iu/ه Bu/س Iu/س Iu/ى Iu/ل Eu/م Iu/ق Bu/ى Eu/ش Au/د Au/ؤ Au/ر Au/ه Bu/ه
ه/Iu Iu/ل Iu/ك Iu/ه Iu/چ Iu/ى Iu/ل Iu/ى Eu/ك Au/ى Au/د Au/ه Su.

Fig. 2. Sentences after tagged

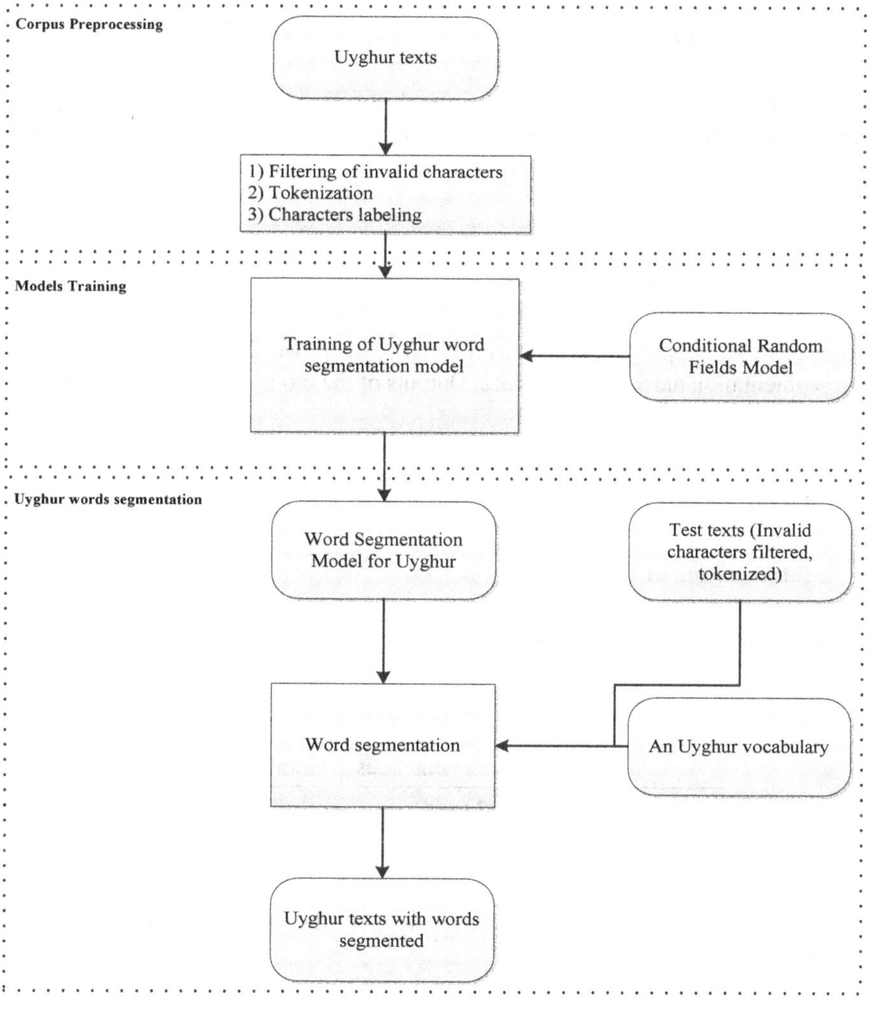

Fig. 3. Framework of the Uyghur word segmentation model

5   Uyghur Word Segmentation

We consider Uyghur word segmentation as a sequence labeling, which labeled every character in a Uyghur word as Su, Bu, Iu, Eu and Au. The entire Uyghur word segmentation system can be described as three parts:

5.1   Corpus Preprocessing

At the first step, the Uyghur texts in training set and test set should be progressed. Such as filtering of invalid characters and words tokenization.

5.2   Models Training

We label the Uyghur texts in training set with Su, Bu, Iu, Eu and Au, respectively. Then, we train the Uyghur word segmentation model with the CRFs model, and the input of model's training are labeled Uyghur texts. To reach a high performance, the training can take several times.

5.3   Uyghur Words Segmentation

Accordingly, we preprocess test set as 5.1 and segment words in test set with Uyghur word segmentation model trained in 5.2. Outputs of the model are Uyghur words which segmented.

6   Experiments

6.1   Introduction of Corpus

Corpora used in our experiments are listed as follows:

Table 1. Statistic of Corpora

	Number of sentences	Number of words
Training Set	12,000	205,814
Test Set	1,121	18,923

Except the separator of stem and suffixes, we labeled stems and suffixes character by character.

6.2   Set up

In this paper, we compare our method with several widely used models, such as HMM, Maximum Entropy et.al. The HMM segmentation model we used here was implemented by ourselves; we use the open source MaxEnt tool[1] which developed by Le Zhang as the training tool for Maximum Entropy segmentation model. Our method is based on CRFs; we use the CRF++[2], also an open source developed with C++ as our baseline.

Before models training, we preprocess the training set and test set used in experiments; include tokenization, invalid characters deletion, and et.al.

In this paper, we evaluate word segmentation results by P_r (Recall), P_p (Precision) and F-score. P_p is the number of correct results divided by the number of all returned results. P_r is the number of correct results divided by the number of results that should have been returned. A measure that combines precision and recall is the harmonic mean of precision and recall, the traditional F-measure or balanced F-score:

$$P_p = \frac{tp}{tp + fp}, \ P_r = \frac{tp}{tp + fn}, F_{score} = \frac{2 * P_p * P_r}{P_p + P_r} \tag{2}$$

6.3   Analysis of Experimental Results

Table 2. Evaluation of Uyghur word segmentation models

Models	Scores		
	Precision (%)	**Recall (%)**	**F-score (%)**
FSM	78.32	72.50	75.30
HMM	85.01	84.32	84.66
MaxEnt	90.14	89.70	89.92
CRFs	93.22	90.58	91.88
CRFs + VOC	94.20	91.17	92.66

---

[1] http://homepages.inf.ed.ac.uk/lzhang10/maxent_toolkit.html
[2] https://code.google.com/p/crfpp/

Because lack of disambiguation ability, the FSM (Finite State Machine) segmentation model got the lowest score among five models; The HMM (Hidden Markov Model) can be understood as a CRF (Conditional Random Fields) with very specific feature functions that use constant probabilities to model state transitions and emissions, so its performance is better than FSM, but a little lower than MaxEnt (Maximum Entropy). Compare with CRFs (Conditional Random Fields) and CRFs + VOC (CRFs with a Uyghur vocabulary), the segmentation quality of the MaxEnt Model relatively weak, that is may because the MaxEnt mode only optimized locally. The CRFs model loosely be understood as a generalization of an HMM that makes the constant transition probabilities into arbitrary functions that vary across the positions in the sequence of hidden states, also, we labeled the training set based on characters rather than words, which provided more information inner Uyghur words, therefore, the CRFs and the CRFs + VOC outperformed other three models in Uyghur segmentation. For corrected errors during segmenting, we also used an Uyghur vocabulary in these experiments.

7   Conclusion

In this paper, we present a novel Uyghur word segmentation method, which consider the Uyghur word segmentation as a sequence labeling problem, rather than labeled sequence as word-based, we label the training set as character-based. Experimental show that our method outperforms other traditional methods significantly. In our feature work, we will import more features into the training of Uyghur word segmentation model, and extend our method to other languages.

Acknowledgements. This work is supported by the Strategic Priority Research Program of the Chinese Academy of Sciences (Grant No.XDA06030400), West Light Foundation of Chinese Academy of Sciences (Grant No.LHXZ201301 XBBS201216), the Xinjiang High-Tech Industrialization Project (Grant No. 201412101) and Young Creative Sci-Tech Talents Cultivation Project of Xinjiang Uyghur Autonomous Region (Grant No. 2013731021).

References

1. Christopher, D.M., Hinrich, S.: Foundations of Statistical Natural Language Processing. MIT Press, Cambridge (1999)
2. Meystre, S., Haug, P.J.: Automation of a problem list using natural language processing. BMC Medical Informatics and Decision Making 5(1), 30 (2005)
3. Collobert, R., Weston, L., Bottou, M., Karlen, K.K., Kuksa, P.: Natural Language Processing (Almost) from Scratch. Journal of Machine Learning Research 12, 2493–2537 (2011)
4. Zaokere, K., Aishan, W., Tuergen, Y., et al.: Uyghur noun stemming system based on hybrid method. Computer Engineering and Applications 49(1), 171–175 (2013)
5. Zou, Y., Tuergen, Y., Mairehaba, A., Aishan, W., Parida, T.: Uyghur event-anchored temporal expressions recognition using stemming method. Computer Engineering and Design 35(2), 625–630 (2014)

6. Xue, H., Dong, X., Wang, L., Osman, T., Jiang, T.: Unsupervised Uyghur word segmentation method based on affix corpus. Computer Engineering and Design 32(9), 3191–3194 (2011)
7. Chen, P.: Uyghur Stem Segmentation and POS Tagging based on Corpora. Master's Thesis, Xinjiang University (2006)
8. Adongbieke, G., Ablimit, M.: Research on Uighur Word Segmentation. Journal of Chinese Information Processing 18(6), 61–65 (2004)
9. Lafferty, J., McCallum, A., Pereira, F.: Conditional random fields: Probabilistic models for segmenting and labeling sequence data (2001)
10. Sha, F., Pereira, F.: Shallow parsing with conditional random fields. In: Proceedings of the Conference of the North American Chapter of the Association for Computational Linguistics on Human Language Technology, vol. 1, pp. 134–141. Association for Computational Linguistics (2003)
11. Wallach, H.M.: Conditional random fields: An introduction. Technical Reports (CIS), 22 (2004)
12. Morwal, S., Jahan, N., Chopra, D.: Named entity recognition using hidden Markov model (HMM). Int. J. Nat. Lang. Comput(IJNLC) 1(4), 15–23 (2012)
13. Morwal, S., Chopra, D.: NERHMM: A Tool For Named Entity Recognition based on Hidden Markov Model. International Journal on Natural Language Computing (IJNLC) 2, 43–49 (2013)
14. Ratnaparkhi, A.: A simple introduction to maximum entropy models for natural language processing. IRCS Technical Reports Series 81 (1997)
15. Berger, A.L., Pietra, V.J.D., Pietra, S.A.D.: A maximum entropy approach to natural language processing. Computational Linguistics 22(1), 39–71 (1996)
16. Malouf, R.: A comparison of algorithms for maximum entropy parameter estimation. In: Proceedings of the 6th Conference on Natural Language Learning, vol. 20, pp. 1–7. Association for Computational Linguistics (2002)
17. Ratnaparkhi, A.: A maximum entropy model for part-of-speech tagging. In: Proceedings of the Conference on Empirical Methods in Natural Language Processing, vol. 1, pp. 133–142 (1996)

Analysis of the Chinese -- Portuguese Machine Translation of Chinese Localizers *Qian* and *Hou*

Chunhui Lu, Ana Leal, Paulo Quaresma, and Márcia Schmaltz

University of Macau, Macau S.A.R., China
{olivio.lu,analuleal}@gmail.com,
pq@di.uevora.pt, marcias@umac.mo

Abstract. The focus of the present article is the two Chinese localizers *qian* (front) and *hou* (back), in their function of time, in the process of the Chinese-Portuguese machine translation, and is integrated in the project *Autema SynTree* (annotation and Analysis of Bilingual Syntactic Trees for Chinese/Portuguese). The text corpus used in the research is composed of 46 Chinese texts, extracted from The International Chinese Newsweekly, identified as source text (ST), and target texts (TT) are composed of translations into Portuguese executed by the Portuguese-Chinese Translator (PCT) and humans. In Portuguese the prepositions of transversal axis such as *antes de* and *depois de*, are used to indicate the time before and after, corresponding to *qian* and *hou* in Chinese. Nevertheless, inconsistencies related to the translation of the localizers are found in the output of the PCT when comparing it with the human translation (HT). Based thereupon, the present article shows the developed syntax rules to solve the inconsistencies found in the PCT output. The translations and the proposed rules were evaluated through the application of BLEU metrics.

Keywords: Machine translation, Chinese, Portuguese, Chinese localizer, BLEU.

1 Introduction

The present work was developed in the ambit of machine translation with the main object of contributing to solve the inconsistencies found in the process and those detected in the output of the PCT System[1], as well as to improve the performance of the same system. The PCT system was developed to satisfy the increasing demand for translating tools to serve the dual official language needs of the Territory of Macau. It is a rule-based system and applies the scheme of annotation in syntax trees in the representation of bilingual examples and the Constraint Synchronous Grammar (Wong et al, 2012).

The present article is part of the *Autema Syntree* project, whose aim is to find solutions in terms of rules and syntax heuristics in order to solve inconsistencies in

---

[1] Chinese-Portuguese Machine Translation System, developed by the University of Macau (Wong et al., 2010).

X. Shi and Y. Chen (Eds.): CWMT 2014, CCIS 493, pp. 70–79, 2014.
© Springer-Verlag Berlin Heidelberg 2014

Chinese - Portuguese machine translated texts. The inconsistencies were observed in the output that has been analyzed in the text corpus of the *AuTema-Dis II* [2] project, translated by the PCT.

The initiative to carry on this work came in result of Liu's Master's Degree Dissertation (2013), which was also produced within the context of the *Autema SynTree* project. She presents a contrasting analysis of machine translation of adverbial phrases of time, from Chinese to Portuguese, and proposes certain grammar rules to improve PCT performance. The focus of the present work is to analyze the localizer phrases that appear as adverbials of time in the syntax, in a continuation and a specification of the study made by Liu (2013).

According to Chinese grammar, localizers are words that indicate a certain direction or a relative positional relationship. They are divided into two categories according to their composition: simple localizers and compound localizers (Liu, 2004: 50). Simple localizers are monosyllabic, as, for example, *shang* 上 (up), *xia* 下 (down), *qian* 前 (front) and *hou* 后 (back). This research focuses on *qian* 前 and *hou* 后 as elements that indicate previous and future time.

BLEU, acronym for Bilingual Evaluation Understudy, is an evaluation metric for machine translation. The use of this metric offers certain advantages such as high efficiency, low cost, independence of languages and strict correlation with human evaluation (Papineni, K., et al, 2002). In the present research, the test BLEU was applied in the evaluation of the translation made by the PCT and the texts post-edited with proposed new syntax rules, duly implemented.

In the next section, we present the methodology chosen for this work; in section 3 we make the theoretical review related to the Chinese localizers with emphasis on *qian* and *hou*, as well as the translation of both localizers in Portuguese. In section 4 we present an analysis of the data gathered from our corpus and we propose four syntax rules to be applied to the system in order to contribute to the solution of the inconsistencies found and towards improving the PCT performance. In section 5 we describe the results of the BLEU testing. In the last section we present the conclusions reached in this study and some of the possibilities for future works.

2   Methodology

The present work involves two areas that are complementary: Linguistics and Computer Science. The area of linguistics relates to the grammar and syntax processes that characterize both Chinese and Portuguese languages, while the area of computer science relates to the use of the PCT and the application of the BLEU algorithm.

The present research adopts the following methodology:

1. Analysis of the source text (ST), namely the 46 Chinese texts, extracted from the *International Chinese Newsweekly*, with the marking of all localizers found.

---

[2] Automatization of Discursive Thematic Analysis (AuTema-Dis II), research grant of the University of Macau RG035/09-10s/ALL/FSH.

2. Analysis of the distribution of all marked localizers, for statistical assessment of their occurrence in the ST.
3. Classification of the marked localizers into two categories: simple localizers and compound localizers.
4. Analysis of the syntax function of the localizer phrases (phrases or sentences where the localizers are present and related to) in the ST.
5. Identification of localizer phrases of *qian* and *hou* in the target text translated by the PCT Machine Translator (PCT MT) and comparison with the human translation (HT) according to syntax structure.
6. Identification and categorization of inconsistencies found in the PCT MT.
7. Proposal of syntax rules to solve inconsistencies.
8. Application of BLEU testing for evaluation of PCT MT and the texts post-edited according to the syntax rules.
9. Evaluation of the proposed rules through the application of the BLEU metric.

3   Literature Review

According to Chao (1979:278), Chinese localizers are used to indicate place and time position. In Chinese grammar they are classified under the subject category, and are equivalent to prepositions when translated to a western language, as in the case of Portuguese.

In what concerns the relationship between the Chinese localizer and the preposition in a western language, Shen (1984) makes a comparison: "the prepositions of place in Chinese are always combined with localizers, while in English the sense of place is already included in the prepositions (and does not need to use localizers). For example, the syntax structure "preposition + noun", in English, is equivalent to "preposition + noun + localizer", in Chinese (...). In many cases the prepositions are omitted". In other words, to indicate place or time, the localizer in Chinese has the same semantic function as the English preposition. Portuguese, the target language of our corpus, which originates from the European family, is also within the framework of Shen's (1984) study.

The present research is dedicated to Chinese-Portuguese machine translation and aims to verify the relationship between the Chinese localizer and the Portuguese preposition, in function of time, focusing on the two temporal localizers *qian* and *hou* in Chinese and in Portuguese.

3.1   Chinese Localizer

In what concerns the Chinese localizer, we have chosen the definitions made by Zhu and Yuan. Zhu (2007:40) categorizes localizers in two types: simple localizers and compound localizers; "the simple localizers include *shang* 上 (up), *xia* 下 (down), *qian* 前 (front), *hou* 后 (back), *li* 里 (within), *wai* 外 (outside), *nei* 内 (inside), *zhong* 中 (center), *zuo* 左 (left), *you* 右 (right), *dong* 东 (east), *xi* 西 (west), *nan*

南 (south), *bei* 北 (north). The compound localizer is a combination of the simple localizer plus a suffix such as *bian* (*er*) 边儿, *mian* (*er*) 面儿, *tou* (*er*) 头儿 "[3].

According to Yuan (2010: 58), simple localizers are analyzed from the standpoint of quantity, they are limited and they may be counted; from the standpoint of dependency they are "adhesive words"[4] and cannot function independently from the structure. In what concerns their position in the structure, localizers are considered postpositional "adhesive words", because they are associated with a nominal component forming a localizer phrase.

In what concerns grammar function, localizers may "be joined" with nouns or phrases, forming new localizer phrases to indicate the place, time, range and limits (Liu, 2010:122), working in the phrase as subject, object, attribute and adverbial (Qiu, 2008: 279).

Let us see the following examples: the localizer (LC) *zhōng* 中 is postpositional to the nominal phrase (NP) 其家 (*sua casa*) forming a localizing phrase (LCP) with the function of indicating a certain place (ex.1). The localizer *hòu* 后 is postpositional to the nominal phrase (NP) 智利地震 (*terremoto do Chile*) forming a localizer phrase by indicating a future time (ex. 2).

Example 1

ST	*zài* *qí* *jiā* *zhōng*
	在/P 其/Pron 家/N 中/LC
Interlinear translation	*em / sua / casa / centro...*
Syntax structure	(PP (P 在) (LCP (NP其家) (LC中)))
HT	*na sua casa*

Example 2

ST	*zhìlì* *dìzhèn* *hòu*
	智利/N 地震/N 后/LC
Interlinear translation	*Chile / terremoto / atrás...*
Syntax structure	(LCP (NP智利地震) (LC后))
HT	*depois do terremoto do Chile...*

---

[3] The present article deals mainly with simple localizers, as the percentage of their appearance in our corpus is significant.

[4] According to Yuan, the simple localizer belongs to the "adhesive words" 黏着词 classification, as it only makes sense when associated with a word that has a fix meaning.

3.2   *Qian* (front) and *hou* (back) Temporal in Chinese and Portuguese

According to the Chinese grammar, both *qian* and *hou* have not only temporal function but also location function. However, as shown in our corpus, the location function is not within the scope of the present study - we debate *qian* and *hou* exclusively in its temporal function.

Lü (1999) made an intervention concerning the grammar function of temporal *qian* and *hou*. The localizer phrases of *qian* indicate, usually, an event that happens earlier in relation to a certain point of reference. On the contrary, the localizer phrases containing *hou* indicate usually an event that occurs later in relation to a reference point. However, the forms of composing the localizer phrases are the same: (1) noun/nominal phrase + *qian (hou)*; (2) verb/verbal phrase + *qian (hou)*; (3) sentence + *qian (hou)*.

In Portuguese some prepositions (simple preposition and compound preposition/prepositional phrase) may be used to manifest a spatial and temporal relationship, such as affirmed by Castilho (2012: 585 - 586): "accepting that the prepositions locate the figure in relation to a certain point of reference, thus its basic meaning may be captured through the following axis (...) transversal spatial axis: previous localization (*antes, antes de, diante de, em frente de...*), posterior localization (*atrás de, por trás de, após, depois de*). Time category is connected to this axis, associating the space in front of us imagetically to the future towards which we are directed, and to the past the posterior space, whereof we are getting away".

4   Analysis

As we mentioned, our corpus is composed of 46 Chinese texts, extracted from The International Chinese Newsweekly, identified as source text (ST) and the respective translations into Portuguese were made by the PCT machine and by humans.

According to the statistics, localizers were found in 32 of the 46 texts. The number of ST where localizers appear represents a percentage of 69.6%, which represents a high frequency of occurrence, as may be confirmed in Table 1, hereunder.

Table 1. Distribution of localizers in the ST

	Number of texts	Percentage
ST where localizers appear	32	69.6%
ST where localizers do not appear	14	30.4%
Total	46	100%

On the ST a total of 54 localizers were found, including 47 simple localizers and 7 compound localizers. From these statistics, it is evident that the number of simple localizers represents a larger number of occurrences, around 87%. In order to remain focused and for the sake of specification, the present article refers only to the simple localizers. See Table 2.

Table 2. ST Localizers Category

	Number	Percentage
Simple localizers	47	87.0%
Compound localizers	7	13.0%
Total	54	100%

In Table 3, the simple localizers that appear in the corpus were organized and counted. Amongst them, *hou* (back) and *zhong* (center) appear with great frequency (29.8% and 27.7%), followed by *shang* (up) (14.9%), *qian* (front) (12.8%) and *nei* (inside) (6.4%). In the present research we focus exclusively on the following two localizers: *qian* and *hou* (for a total of 20, representing a percentage of 42.6%).

Table 3. ST Simple localizers

Simple localizers	Number	Percentage
qian 前 (front)	6	12.8%
hou 后 (back)	14	29.8%
shang 上 (up)	7	14.9%
zhong 中 (center)	13	27.7%
xia 下 (down)	2	4.3%
wai 外 (outside)	1	2.1%
nei 内 (inside)	3	6.4%
jian 间 (between)	1	2.1%
Total	47	100%

Example 3 is a localizer phrase (LCP) with the localizer (LC) *qian* postpositional in relation to the verbal phrase (VP), whose structure is "VP + LC". See the human translation (HT) that is a prepositional phrase (PP) initiated by the preposition (P) *antes de*, composed of "P + VP". However, the text translated by the PCT (PCT MT), does not show a grammar structure and does not contain valid semantic content, because the localizer *qian* was literally translated as "*em frente*".

Example 3

ST	*Bèilǔ*	*qián*
	被掳/V	前/LC
Interlinear translation	*ser raptado / frente*	
ST Syntax structure	(LCP (VP (V被掳)) (LC前))	
PCT MT	**ser aprisionar em frente*	
HT	*antes de ser raptada*	
HT Syntax structure	(PP (P *antes de*) (VP *ser raptada*))	

We find that the ST in the following three examples are localizer phrases (LCP) of *hou*, although in different syntax structures. Example 4 is composed of "nominal phrase (NP) + localizer (LC)", while the HT in Portuguese is a prepositional phrase (PP) composed of "P + NP". The structure of the ST in example 5 is "VP+LC", and the structure of the relevant translation is "P+VP", therefore a prepositional phrase (PP).

Example 6 is relatively more complex because the source text is a localizer phrase (LCP), composed of a sentence (S) and a localizer (LC). The sentence (S) includes the subject "总统马英九 (*presidente Ma Yingjeou*)" and the predicate "上台 (*tomar posse*)". See in Portuguese HT the prepositional phrase (PP) composed of the simple preposition *após* and the nominal phrase (NP) (*a posse do presidente Ma Yingjeou*).

Example 4

ST	*zhìlì*	*dìzhèn*	*hòu*
	智利 /N	地震/N	后 /LC
Interlinear translation	*Chile / terremoto /atrás*		
ST syntax structure	(LCP (NP (N智利) (N地震)) (LC后))		
PCT MT	**o terremoto de Chile atrás de*		
HT	*depois do terremoto do Chile*		
HT syntax structure	(PP (P *depois de*) (NP *o terremoto do Chile*))		

Example 5

ST	*shōugòu* *yǒubāng* *hòu* 收购 /V 友邦 /N 后/LC
Interlinear translation	*comprar / AIA / atrás*
ST syntax structure	(LCP (VP (V收购) (N友邦)) (LC后))
PCT MT	**adquire AIA atrás de*
HT	*depois de ter comprado a AIA*
HT syntax structure	(PP (P *depois de*) (VP *ter comprado a AIA*))

Example 6

ST	*zǒngtǒng* *mǎyīngjiǔ* *shàngtái* *hòu* 总统 /N 马英九/N 上台/V 后 /LC
Interlinear translation	*presidente / Ma Yingjeou / tomar posse / trás*
ST syntax structure	(LCP (S (NP 总统马英九) (V 上台)) (LC 后))
PCT MT	**Ma Yingjeou do presidente tomar posse atrás de*
HT	*após a posse do presidente Ma Yingjeou*
HT syntax structure	(PP (P *após*) (NP *a posse do presidente Ma Yingjeou*))

We find that the Chinese localizers, as we referred to in section 3, are equivalent to the Portuguese prepositions that indicate place and time. As for the syntax level, a localizer phrase in Chinese normally corresponds to a prepositional phrase in Portuguese. In our case, the prepositions of transversal spatial axis such as *antes de*, *depois de*, *após* are used to indicate previous and future time, corresponding to the localizers *qian* and *hou* in Chinese.

Nevertheless, when processing phrases with a Chinese localizer, the PCT does not manage to identify or use the differences between both languages and translates word by word. From the inconsistencies we found, we suggest the following rules that are intended to be used in post-editing of the Chinese-Portuguese machine translation of *qian* and *hou* temporal:

Table 4. Syntax Rules proposed

	Chinese	Portuguese	Meaning
1	VP + *qian* Ex. *beilu / qian*	*Antes de* + VP Ex. *antes de ser raptada*	Previous time
2	NP + *hou* Ex. *zhili / dizhen / hou*	*Após* + NP / *Depois de* + NP Ex. *após / depois de o terremoto do Chile*	Future time
3	VP + *hou* Ex. *shougou / Youbang / hou*	*Depois de* + VP Ex. *depois de ter comprado a AIA*	Future time
4	S + *hou* Ex. *zongtong / Ma Ying-jeou / shangtai / hou*	*Após* + NP / *Depois de* + NP Ex. *após / depois de a posse do presidente Ma Yingjeou*	Future time

5   BLEU Testing Results

BLEU is a metric to evaluate machine translation developed due to the difficulty to make an objective human evaluation with quantitative values. To evaluate the quality of a machine translation, the principle is to measure its proximity towards one or more human translation used as reference and the nearer it is to the human translation, the better the machine translation will be. BLEU requires two metrics: the numeric method to evaluate the proximity; high quality human translation to be a reference (Papineni, K., et al, 2002).

The present work introduces a research dedicated to the analysis of localizers in the process of machine translation and is dedicated to improve the PCT. However, an efficient method of evaluation is necessary to verify with precision the PCT output and the post-edition of texts according to the rules proposed in section 4. From the comparison of both results generated through the BLEU metric, it is possible to highlight the difference and to verify the efficiency of the rules proposed and implemented in the system.

As described in Table 1, the number of ST where localizers appear is 32. However, the present research analyses exclusively the translation of the two Chinese localizers *qian* and *hou* that appear in 16 ST. In this manner, the 16 ST and the 16 texts post-edited with syntax rules constitute the aim of the present BLEU testing, using human translations as reference.

The online system ibleu[5] was used to perform our test. The result of the PCT MT is 41.75 (baseline) and the post edition is 42.20 (the value of the ibleu is between 0 and 100, the higher the value the better the translation), which marks a significant increase and in

---

[5] https://code.google.com/p/ibleu/

general terms confirms a better quality to the machine translation, as well as to the efficiency of the implemented syntax rules.

6   Conclusion and Future Works

We introduced in this article the two Chinese localizers *qian* and *hou* within the ambit of the Portuguese-Chinese machine translation. The corpus of our research shows that the PCT system cannot generate a correct translation of Chinese localizers, performing a literal translation. Through the analysis of the corpus and grammar comparison of the two languages, we find that the localizers such as *qian* and *hou* in function of time are generated as prepositions of transversal spatial axis in Portuguese such as *antes de*, *depois de* and *após*, to indicate previous and future time. Based on the results, we proposed the four syntax rules introduced in section 4, which were implemented in post-editing of PCT MT and later evaluated through the BLEU metric, showing a significant improvement in machine generated translations.

As shown in Table 3, besides *qian* and *hou*, there are 6 other types of localizers that appear in the ST, which are already being analyzed and shall be later introduced in the continuation of this work.

References

1. Castilho, A.T.: New Grammar of Brazilian Portuguese. Editora Contexto, São Paulo (2012) (in Portuguese)
2. Chao, Y.R.: A Grammar of Spoken Chinese. University of California Press, Berkeley (1968)
3. Liu, J.Y.: Practical Chinese Grammar. History and Philosophy Press, Taipei (2010) (in Chinese)
4. Lü, S.X.: Eight Hundred Words of Modern Chinese Language. Commercial Press, Beijing (1999) (in Chinese)
5. Liu, S.Y.: Chinese-Portuguese Machine Translation: Analysis of Temporal Adverbial Phrases. Master Thesis of University of Macau (2013) (in Portuguese)
6. Liu, Y.H., Pan, W.Y., Gu, W.: Chinese Grammar. Commercial Press, Beijing (2004) (in Chinese)
7. Papineni, K., Roukos, S., Ward, T., Zhu, W.J.: BLEU: a method for automatic evaluation of machine translation. In: Proceedings of the 40th Annual Meeting on Association for Computational Linguistics, pp. 311–318 (2002)
8. Qiu, B.: Research on related issues of Chinese orientation words. Academia Press, Shanghai (2008) (in Chinese)
9. Shen, J.X.: A contrastive study of English and Chinese prepositions. Foreign Language Teaching and Research 2, 1–8 (1984)
10. Vilela, M.: Portuguese Grammar. Livraria Almedina, Coimbra (1995) (in Portuguese)
11. Wong, F., Chao, S.: PCT: Portuguese-Chinese Machine Translation Systems. Journal of Translation Studies 13(1-2), 181–196 (2010)
12. Wong, F., Oliveira, F., Li, Y.P.: Hybrid Machine Aided Translation System based on Constraint Synchronous Grammar and Translation Corresponding Tree. Journal of Computers 7(2), 309–316 (2012)
13. Yuan, Y.L.: A Cognitive Investigation and Fuzzy Classification of Word-class in Mandarin Chinese. Shanghai Educational Publishing House, Shanghai (2010) (in Chinese)
14. Zhu, D.X.: Teaching Material of Chinese Grammar. Commercial Press, Hong Kong (2007) (in Chinese)

Chunk-Based Dependency-to-String Model
with Japanese Case Frame

Jinan Xu[*], Peihao Wu, Jun Xie, and Yujie Zhang

[1] School of Computer and Information Technology, Beijing Jiaotong University,
Beijing 100044, China
[2] Beijing Samsung Telecom R&D Center, Beijing 100028, China
{jaxu,12120465}@bjtu.edu.cn, j0907.xie@samsung.com
yjzhang @bjtu.edu.cn

Abstract. This paper proposes an idea to integrate Japanese case frame into chunk-based dependency-to-string model. At first, case frames are acquired from Japanese chunk-based dependency analysis results. Then case frames are used to constraint rule extraction and decoding in chunk-based dependency-to-string model. Experimental results show that the proposed method performs well on long structural reordering and lexical translation, and achieves better performance than hierarchical phrase-based model and word-based dependency-to-string model on Japanese to Chinese test sets.

Keywords: Statistical Machine Translation; Japanese Case Frame; syntax structure; chunk-based dependency-to-string model.

1 Introduction

Agglutinative languages have an essential and complicated syntactical difference problem with other languages. For instance, Japanese is standard agglutinative language, and it's a subject-object-verb (SOV) language, which is very different from English and Chinese. Also, Japanese case frames are dominance and the suffixes of Japanese verbs describes the tense of Japanese sentences. All these characteristics bring out the poor performance in translations between agglutinative languages.

In solving problems of syntactical differences, researchers propose enormous syntax translation models. Such as, syntax tree-to-string models(Yamada K 2001, Liu Y et al., 2006), forest-to-string models(Liu Y et al., 2006, Mi H et al., 2008) and dependency-to-string model(Xie J et al., 2011). However, these models should be modified before they are applied to Japanese machine translation, according to syntax structure difference between Japanese and other languages.

Traditional Japanese machine translation focuses on improving the performance of Japanese-English machine translation. Researchers propose a chunk-based Japanese-to-English statistical machine translation (Watanabe T et al., 2003). The procedure of this idea is shown below. At first, chunks of each source sentence are acquired. Then,

---

[*] Corresponding author.

X. Shi and Y. Chen (Eds.): CWMT 2014, CCIS 493, pp. 80–92, 2014.

chunks are translated separately. Finally, a chunk-based reordering model is used to reorder the order of chunks, and get the final translation. However, Japanese syntax structure is not used to handle the syntax structure difference between languages.

A manually set method is proposed to ease syntax structure difference problem (Hoshino S et al., 2013). This method transforms Japanese syntax structure into the structure of English before translating. This method depends on languages and fields, and its rules are defined by strong subjectivity. All shortcomings make this method unable to be promoted.

The other way to solve syntax structure difference problem is to acquire reordering rules automatically. Researchers propose a way of using head-driven syntax tree and the alignment of parallel corpus to acquire reordering rules (Wu X et al., 2011a). This method acquires rules in linear time. It transform original tree into transformed tree with bottom-to-up method, and reorder English sentences into Japanese orders. Experimental results prove that this method can improve the results of Japanese-to-English machine translation. Also, acquiring rules from chunk-based dependency tree is raised (Wu X et al., 2011b). At first, Japanese dependency trees are transformed into head-driven syntax tree to extract pre-ordering rules. However, all methods shown above do not integrate syntax tree information into translation model.

A method of integrating syntax tree information into translation model gains significant improvement (Wu D et al., 2009). This method has two passes; the first pass is performed using a conventional phrase-based SMT model. The second pass is performed by a reordering strategy guided by shallow semantic parsers that produce both semantic frame and role labels. The performance of this method is constricted by the performance of existing phrase-based model, and it has lots of difficulties in Japanese machine translation.

In order to make use of Japanese syntax information in SMT. This paper proposes an idea of integrating Japanese case frame into chunk-based dependency-to-string model. At first, case frames are acquired from Japanese chunk-based dependency analysis results. Then case frames are used to constraint rule extraction and decoding in chunk-based dependency-to-string model. Experimental results prove that the proposed method could ease the problem of syntax difference between languages and improve the performance of machine translation.

The reminder of this paper is organized as follows. Section 2 briefly reviews the related studies on case grammar and Japanese case frame. The novel chunk-based dependency-to-string model is proposed in section 3. Section 4 describes the decoder procedure of the proposed method. Section 5 reports the experimental results and analysis. Section 6 concludes this paper with our prospects for future work.

2   Case Grammar and Japanese Case Frame

2.1   Case Grammar

According to Fillmore, each verb selects a certain number of deep cases which form its case frame. Thus, a case frame describes important aspects of semantic valency, of verbs, adjectives and nouns[1].

---

[1] http://en.wikipedia.org/wiki/Case_grammar

Case grammar describes what kind of nouns are related to verbs, and each noun has a unique relationship with each verb.. It indicates the skeletons of sentences, and exposits the deep syntax and semantic information of sentences. Therefore, case grammar plays an important role in natural language processing. However, so far, case grammar is not efficiently applied in statistical machine translation.

2.2   Case Grammar

Japanese is a typical agglutinative, it belongs to classical case frame grammar language. As Japanese case frames are dominant in sentences, we can easily distinguish them from other parts of the sentence. Fig 1(a) shows an example of chunk-based dependency tree.

Japanese case particles (Table 1) are dominant. It's easy to distinguish each component of syntax structure in a sentence. For example, a Japanese sentence "彼は本を右手で持つ (He takes the book with the right hand) ". The case frame of the verb "持つ" is composed of three parts except for itself, the subject "彼は", the object "本を" and the instrument "右手で". In this case, it contains a deep case frame with three particles "は(ha)", "を(wo)" and "で(de)". The dependency tree of this sentence is shown in Fig 1(a). Fig 1(b) shows the case frame of this sentence.

Until now, Japanese parsers keep a good performance such as KNP (Jan et al., 2009). For large-scale lexicalized Japanese case frame is used to improve the performance of Japanese syntax parsers, and it's easily extracted from the web using semi-supervised learning (Kawahara et al., 2006a, 2006b; Sasano et al., 2011).

Particles Types	Morphology
Subject / Agent	が (ga)、は (ha)
Object	を (wo)、に (ni)、〜(he)
Instrument	に (ni)、で (de)
Experience	に (ni)、と (to)
Source	に (ni)、〜(he) 、から (kara) 、より (yori)、で (de) 、の (no)
Goal	に (ni)、〜(he)
Location	に (ni)、から (kara)、より (yori)、で (de)
Time	に (ni)、から (kara)、より (yori)、で (de)

Fig. 1. Parts of Japanese case particles types

Table 1. The dependency tree and deep case frame of verb "持つ"

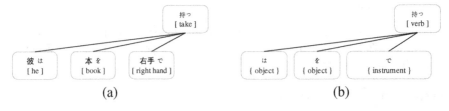

(a)   (b)

2.3   The Definition of Japanese Case Frame

In this paper, three tuple $<V,C,R>$ is used to describe the definition of Japanese case frame.

Where,

V represents word prototype of Japanese predicates, which is different from Japanese conjugation.

C represents the conjugation set of Japanese predicates; conjugations of verbs describe tense, imperative, assumption etc. Table 2 shows some conjugations of Japanese verb "持つ".

Table 2. Conjugations of Japanese verb "持つ"

verb conjunction	基本形	未然形	意志形	タ形
japanese	持つ	持た	持とう	持った
english	take	going to take	want to take	have taken

R is the set of Japanese particles (shown in Table 3). In Japanese, Some adverb auxiliary words, such as "は"、"では"and"には"also have the characteristics of Japanese particles.

Table 3. Parts of Japanese particles

表層格	ガ格	ヲ格	ニ格	カラ格	ヘ格	ト格	デ格
Particles	が	を	に	から	へ	と	で

Case frame (CF) for Japanese predicates (including verbs, adjective etc.) can be described as a three tuple $<h,t,\varphi>$.

Where,

$h \in V$ is the stem or prototype of a Japanese predicates.

$t \in C$ is the conjugation of predicates in sentences.

$\varphi \in R^*$ is all particles in a certain predicate's case frame, and they are all sorted in the order of their position in the original Japanese sentence.

2.4   Japanese Case Frame Automatically Extraction

For a Japanese chunk-based dependency tree, a predicate can be obtained from the root node of the dependency tree. The CF of predicate in this sentence can be acquired in two ways:

1. CF can be acquired by analyzing chunks which directly depend on the chunk of predicates. The particles in each chunk are obtained by pattern match, and get final CF. In figure 1(a), particles "は", "で"and"を"depends on predicate "持つ", the surface particles are "ガ格", "デ格"and"ヲ格".

2. Also, Japanese case frame dataset[2] is applied to acquire CF. This method can omit the missing of particles in Japanese sentences, so that, the CF is completely acquired. Table 4 presents an example of Japanese case frame dataset.

Table 4. Lexical Japanese Case Frame of predicate "持つ"

Particles	Lexical Word Examples
<ガ格>	人, 子供, 方, <u>彼</u>, 自分, 皆
<ヲ格>	武器 , 銃 , <u>本</u>, 兵器 , 杖 , 拳銃
<デ格>	手 , <u>右手</u> , 両手, 腕, 左腕, 逆手

If multiple CFs are found in method 2, method 1 is used to calculate the similarities for all CFs to obtain the best matched CF.

According to the definition of CF. In Figure 1's sentence, the CF of predicate "持つ" is shown below:

h:持つ   t:基本形   φ:x1:が格,x2:ヲ格,x3:デ格

The expression of this CF is

<持つ, 基本型,   x1:が格,x2:ヲ格,x3:デ格>

3   Chunk-Based Dependency-to-String Model

This paper proposes a method of integrating Japanese case frame into the rule extraction and decoding of chunk-based dependency-to-string model. Case frame is used as a restrictive condition to improve the performance of machine translation.

Three tuple <T,S,A> are used to express sentence pairs. Whereas, T is the source chunk-based dependency tree, S is word sequence of target sentence and A is the word alignment between T and S. Fig 2 illustrates an example of <T,S,A>.

Translation rules in our model include two parts:

Lexical Translation Rules (LTRs). LTRs are used to translate source phrases or chunks into target translation results.

Case Frame Reordering Rules (CFRs). CFRs are used to transform source dependency tree to target sequence. In the proposed model, the definition of CFRs is a four tuple $<h,t,\varphi,\omega>$, which is an extension of CF. $\omega \in R^{*}$ records the order of φ in target sequence.

The procedure of rule extraction has three steps: 1) tree annotation 2) extractable treelet judgment 3) Rule extraction.

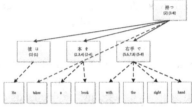

Fig. 2. An illustration of dependency-to-string alignment

---

[2] http://nlp.ist.i.kyoto-u.ac.jp/

3.1   Tree Annotation

Each chunk in chunk-based dependency tree has two properties: 1) alignment span and 2) treelet alignment span.

Definition 1. In each chunk n in chunk-based dependency tree, alignment span $hsp(n)$ stores all target words which have alignment relation with chunk n.

As shown in Figure 2, target words "a" and "book" are aligned to chunk "本 を", therefore, $hsp(本 を) = \{4\text{-}5\}$.

Definition 2. $hsp(n)$ is dependent if chunk n satisfies:

$\forall_{n' \neq n} hsp(n') \cap hsp(n) = \varnothing$

Definition 3. T' is the treelet which root is chunk n. Treelet alignment span $dsp(n)$ includes all alignment points in target words that have alignment relation to T'.

$$dsp(n) = \bigcup_{n' \in T'} hsp(n')$$

In chunk-based dependency tree, alignment span and treelet alignment span for each chunk can be calculated through post-order traversal.

3.2   Extractable Treelet Judgment

Due to word alignment fault and idiom situations, not all case frames in training corpus can be used to extract CFRs. Therefore, each treelet should be judged whether it can used to extract CFRs.

Definition 4. T' is a treelet of T .If root chunk of T' has a predicate, then $T' \in cft(T)$.

Definition 5. Define $adt(T)$ is the set of all extractable treelet. For each $T' \in cft(T)$, if T' satafises the conditions below, then $T' \in adt(T)$. Where, $chunk(h)$ is the chunk which h belongs to three rules.

1. $hsp(chunk(h)) \neq \varnothing$
2. $\forall_{n'} 依存于 \, _{chunk(h)} dsp(n') \neq \emptyset$
3. $dsp(chunk(h))$ is independent in this treelet

In Fig 2, the treelet T' which root is "持つ" satisfies $T' \in cft(T)$. Due to definitions shown below:

$hsp(chunk(持つ)) = hsp(持つ) = \{2\}$ satisfies rule 1 and 3.

$dsp(彼 は) \neq \emptyset, dsp(本 を) \neq \emptyset$ and $dsp(右手 で) \neq \emptyset$ satisfies rule 2.

Therefore, CFR can be extracted from this treelet.

3.3   Rule Extraction

In this paper, translation rules is acquired by up-bottom travel.

3.3.1   LTRs Extraction

In the process of up-bottom travelling, LTRs are extracted according to the two conditions:

- Each chunk in chunk-based dependency tree. For each chunk in dependency tree, LTRs are extracted with parallel word alignment A and source sentence S. The extraction method is based on phrase-based rule extraction (Koehn P et al., 2003).
- If treelet T' ∉adt(T), this treelet will be regarded as a chunk. LTRs will be extracted just same as situation 1.

3.3.2   CFRs Extraction

If treelet T'∈adt(T), the details of CFRs extraction will be described below:

First, treelet alignment span dsp(φ') for each particle φ'∈φ and alignment spanning hsp(h) of predicate h will be acquired.

Then, the order of particles and predicate in target sentence will be determined according to dsp(φ') and hsp(h) and the order is recorded in ω.

After that, a CFR is extracted.

As shown in Figure 2, the case frame order ω of predicate "持つ" in target is ω = x1 h x2 x3. Therefore, The CFR of this case frame is:

<持つ, 基本型, x1:が格,x2:ヲ格,x3:デ格, x1 h x2 x3>

Where, h represents the predicate of this case frame.

3.4   Probability Estimation

The probability estimation of LTRs applies the method of phrase-based rule extraction. The formulation is as follows:

$$P(s|t) = \frac{count(s,t)}{\sum_t count(s,t)} \tag{1}$$

Where,

$P(s|t)$ is the translation probability of source phrase s to target phrase t.

$count(s,t)$ is the co-occurrence times of s and t in training corpus.

Maximum likelihood estimation is introduced to estimate the probability of CFRs. The formulation is shown below:

$$P(< h, t, \varphi, \omega >) = \frac{count(P(<h,t,\varphi,\omega>))}{\sum_{\omega' \in P(<h,t,\varphi,*>)} count(P(<h,t,\varphi,\omega'>))} \tag{2}$$

Where,

$count(P(<h,t,\varphi,\omega>))$ represents the total occurrence times of rule $<h,t,\varphi,\omega>$.

3.5   Modification of CFRs in Statistical Model

According to Japanese case frame dataset, it includes case frames of 34,059 predicates. As the size of training corpus, all CFRs can't be extracted from training corpus. This may lead to a mismatch problem in decoding.

In order to solve the problem of data sparseness. Part-of-speech is used to take over predicates in CFRs. In the definition of CFR $<h,t,\varphi,\omega>$, h is the part-of-speech of the predicate.

After this modification, the original CFR <持つ, 基本型, x1:が格,x2:ヲ格,x3:デ格, x1 x2 h x3> is modified as <子音動詞タ行, 基本型, x1:が格,x2:ヲ格,x3:デ格, x1 h x2 x3>.

4   Model and Decoder

4.1   Model Description

Log-linear model is used as the major model for chunk-base dependency-to-string model. For Japanese chunk-based dependency tree, the best result d^* is calculated from all possible results D.

$$d^*=\text{argmax}_{d \in D}(P(D)) \tag{3}$$

Assume d is the possible way to translate source chunk-based dependency tree into target sentence. The probability of d is defined as follows:

$$P(d) \propto \prod_i \Phi_i(d)^{\lambda i} \tag{4}$$

Where, Φ_i is the parameter of feature i, λ_i is the weight of feature i. The model in our paper has eight parameters.

— The probability of CFRs $P(<h,t,\varphi,\omega>)$
— The probability of LTRs $P(s|t)$和$P(t|s)$
— The lexical probability of LTRs $P_{lex}(s|t)$和$P_{lex}(t|s)$
— Rule penalty $\exp(-1)$
— Word penalty $\exp(|e|)$
— Language model $P_{lm}(e)$

Minimum error rate training (Och F J et al., 2003) is applied to optimize all weights.

4.2   Decoder

Our decoder is based on bottom up chart parsing. Fig 3 illustrates an example of sentence decoding. The main procedure is described in Algorithm 1.

This Algorithm is based on two points:

1. If treelet T'∉adt(T), it should be transformed into word sequences. Then translated this treelet as a chunk with LTRs.
2. If treelet T'∈adt(T), root of T' is translated with LTRs. Then translate all subtrees separately. Finally, all subtrees and roots are reordered and combined to create the final result.

5   Experiment and Data Analysis

5.1   Data Preparation and Tools

Experiments are set up with Japanese-to-Chinese SMT and Japanese-to-English to verify the proposed approach and compare the effectiveness in different language pairs.

Japanese-to-Chinese data includes two different domain tests: news (CWMT2011 Japanese to Chinese corpus) and oral (this corpus is acquired from web). Sentences which could not be parsed are discarded. In news domain, the test and development data of CWMT2011 is used. In oral domain, we randomly extract 1,000 sentences for test data and 1,000 sentences for development data.

Japanese-to-English data includes one domain tests: NTCIR-10 patent Japanese to English data set. According to the dataset, we only report a small data set of NTCIR-10. The statistics of all training set are shown in Table 5.

The statistics of training sets are shown in Table 5.
The configuration of experiments is presented as follows:

- Juman7.0[3]: Japanese word segmenter.
- KNP[4]: Japanese dependency parser.
- Stanford Chinese Segmenter[5]: Chinese word segmenter.
- GIZA++[6] (Och and Ney, 2003): running for word alignments and refines the alignments with "grow-diag-final-and".
- SRI Language Modelling Toolkit[7] (Stolcke, 2002): to establish Chinese 5-gram language model.
- MOSES[8]: training the hierarchical phrase-based baseline system.

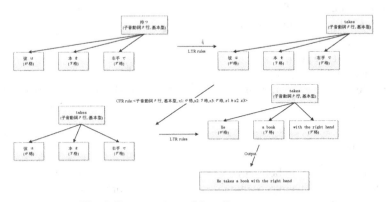

Fig. 3. The procedure of decoding a sentence

[3] http://nlp.ist.i.kyoto-u.ac.jp/index.php?JUMAN
[4] http://nlp.ist.i.kyoto-u.ac.jp/index.php?KNP
[5] http://nlp.stanford.edu/software/segmenter.shtml
[6] http://code.google.com/p/giza-pp/
[7] http://www.speech.sri.com/projects/srilm/
[8] http://www.statmt.org/moses

Decoding Algorithm
Input : Source dependency tree T, LTR rule: L , CFR rule R Output : Translation Result

CFset ← CaseFrame(T)
CFTset ← ACCEPTABLE_CF(T,CFset)
For chunk in T from top to bottom
if chunk ∈ CFTset
then
   translate chunk with L
   translate every subtree which relates to chunk
    reorder subtrees and chunk with R
end
translate subtree as a chunk with L
return the best result of the root chunk

Table 5. Training data sets

		Train	Dev	Test
J2C	news	282,377	498	947
	patent	672,315	2,148	2,107
J2E	patent	300,000	915	1,826

5.2 Experimental Systems

Hierarchical phrase-based model (*hierarchical*) is adopted for comparing the performance of proposed method (*newdep*). The maximum phrase length is given 10 in experiments.

Furthermore, in order to identify whether chunk is valid for dependency-to-string model, the work of (Xie et al., 2011) is used as the dependency-to-string model (*basedep*) in this paper.

5.3 Results

Results in Table 6 shows that the proposed method achieves a better BLEU score than *basedep* in all languages and domains, it proves that the proposed method have a good performance on dependency-to-string model than other models. Furthermore, the size of the proposed method is far less than *hierarchical*. Results also indicate that the proposed method is effective in both Japanese to Chinese and Japanese to English translation directions.

5.4 Analysis

Translation results in J2C and J2E indicate this model has some merits:

Syntax Structural Reordering. Japanese is a typical agglutinative language; its syntax structure is very different from other languages. An example of long distance

Table 6. Experimental Results of Machine Translation

| | Japanese to Chinese | | | | Japanese to english | |
| | news | | Patent | | Patent | |
	rule #	BLEU-4	rule #	BLEU-4	rule #	BLEU-4
newdep	4.2M	**20.82**[*]	40M	**45.14**[*]	19M	**17.93***
hierarchical	25M	20.34	270M	44.54	138M	17.74
basedep	3.8M	16.29	31M	37.91	16M	15.37

syntax structure reordering is shown below. As to the length limitation in rule extraction, *hierarchical* can't extract long distance syntax structure reordering. Meanwhile, our *newdep* model reorders source dependency tree with the help of case frame, and gets relatively high quality reordering results.

Source	[一 次元 の 光 電 素 子 列 を]₁ [用いた 単純な 構成 を]₂ [以下 に 示す。]₃
Reference	[A simple construction using]₂ [a one-dimensional photoelectric element array]₁ [is shown below.]₃
hierarchical	[one-dimensional]₁ [using]₂ [the photoelectric element array]₁ [in a simple structure]₂ [is shown below.]₃
newdep	[a simple structure using]₂ [one-dimensional photoelectric element array]₁ [is shown below.]₃

Lexical word translation. The proposed model uses syntax structure to limit the lexical word translation rule extraction. In the example below, Compared with *HPB*, *newdep* can efficiently reduce the noise of low-quality lexical translation rules. As shown below, the translation of "航空 便" in *newdep* choose a better lexical translation than *hierarchical*.

Source	航空 便 で いくら ぐらい かかり ますか 。
Reference	寄航空 要 多少 钱 ？
hierarchical	用 航空 大约 要 多少 钱 ？
newdep	用 航空 邮寄 要 多少 钱 ？

Parallel Structure Translation. Parallel structure translation is a very complicated problem in machine translation. Japanese sentence has two parallel phrases "ガ ス 噴出孔 ５ ０ から 噴出 し" and "エアバッグ ２ ４ を 展開 さ せる". *HPB* cannot analyze the parallel structure and getwrong translation result.

Source	この ガスは、 ガス 噴出孔 ５ ０ から 噴出 し、 エアバッグ ２ ４ を 展開 さ せる。
Reference	This gas is injected from gas injection ports 50 to extend the air bag 24.
hierarchical	The gas is jetted from the gas ejection holes 50 and the air bag 24 is expanded.
newdep	The gas is jetted from the gas ejection holes 50 to expand the air bag 24.

English syntax structure is closer to Japanese than Chinese. Also, we find J2E translation gets better results than J2C. Especially in the case of parallel structure, J2C can hardly handle this problem, but J2E translates parallel structures in a properly way.

6   Conclusion and Future Work

This paper proposed a chunk-based dependency-to-string model. Case frame is integrated into this model to solve the syntax structure difference problem. Experimental results prove that the proposed model can 1) alleviate structural reordering problem in SMT and 2) evanish useless rule.

The proposed model in this paper is a reference of using semantic information in SMT. As case frame is the first step to Japanese semantic machine translation. In future, case frame will be researched to improve the performance of SMT. New models will also be studied to adapt the proposed syntax tree.

Acknowledgement. The authors were supported by National Nature Science Foundation of China (Contract 61370130) and International Science & Technology Cooperation Program of China under grant   No. 2014DFA11350.

References

1. Yamada, K., Knight, K.: A syntax-based statistical translation model. In: Proceedings of the 39th Annual Meeting on Association for Computational Linguistics, pp. 523–530. Association for Computational Linguistics (2001)
2. Liu, Y., Liu, Q., Lin, S.: Tree-to-string alignment template for statistical machine translation. In: Proceedings of the 21st International Conference on Computational Linguistics and the 44th Annual Meeting of the Association for Computational Linguistics, pp. 609–616. Association for Computational Linguistics (2006)
3. Liu, Y., Huang, Y., Liu, Q., et al.: Forest-to-string statistical translation rules. In: Annual Meeting-Association For Computational Linguistics, vol. 45(1), p. 704 (2007)
4. Mi, H., Huang, L., Liu, Q.: Forest-Based Translation. In: ACL, pp. 192–199 (2008)
5. Xie, J., Mi, H., Liu, Q.: A novel dependency-to-string model for statistical machine translation. In: Proceedings of the Conference on Empirical Methods in Natural Language Processing, pp. 216–226. Association for Computational Linguistics (2011)
6. Watanabe, T., Sumita, E., Okuno, H.G.: Chunk-based statistical translation. In: Proceedings of the 41st Annual Meeting on Association for Computational Linguistics, vol. 1, pp. 303–310. Association for Computational Linguistics (2003)
7. Hoshino, S., Miyao, Y., Sudoh, K., et al.: Two-Stage Pre-ordering for Japanese-to-English Statistical Machine Translation. In: Proceedings of the 6th International Joint Conference on Natural Language Processing (2013)
8. Wu, X., Sudoh, K., Duh, K., et al.: Extracting Pre-ordering Rules from Predicate-Argument Structures. In: IJCNLP, pp. 29–37 (2011)
9. Wu, X., Sudoh, K., Duh, K., et al.: Extracting preordering rules from chunk-based dependency trees for Japanese-to-English translation. In: Proceedings of the 13th Machine Translation Summit, pp. 300–307 (2011)

10. Wu, D., Fung, P.: Semantic roles for smt: a hybrid two-pass model. In: Proceedings of Human Language Technologies: The 2009 Annual Conference of the North American Chapter of the Association for Computational Linguistics, Companion Volume: Short Papers, pp. 13–16. Association for Computational Linguistics (2009)
11. Kawahara, D., Kurohashi, S.: Case frame compilation from the web using high-performance computing. In: Proceedings of the 5th International Conference on Language Resources and Evaluation, pp. 1344–1347 (2006)
12. Kawahara, D., Kurohashi, S.: A fully-lexicalized probabilistic model for Japanese syntactic and case structure analysis. In: Proceedings of the Main Conference on Human Language Technology Conference of the North American Chapter of the Association of Computational Linguistics, pp. 176–183. Association for Computational Linguistics (2006)
13. Sasano, R., Kurohashi, S.: A Discriminative Approach to Japanese Zero Anaphora Resolution with Large-scale Lexicalized Case Frames. In: IJCNLP, pp. 758–766 (2011)
14. Koehn, P., Och, F.J., Marcu, D.: Statistical phrase-based translation. In: Proceedings of the 2003 Conference of the North American Chapter of the Association for Computational Linguistics on Human Language Technology, vol. 1, pp. 48–54. Association for Computational Linguistics (2003)
15. Och, F.J.: Minimum error rate training in statistical machine translation. In: Proceedings of the 41st Annual Meeting on Association for Computational Linguistics, vol. 1, pp. 160–167. Association for Computational Linguistics (2003)

A Novel Hybrid Approach to Arabic Named Entity Recognition

Mohamed A. Meselhi[1], Hitham M. Abo Bakr[1], Ibrahim Ziedan[1], and Khaled Shaalan[2]

[1]Derpartment of Computer and System Engineering; Faculty of Engineering,
Zagazig University, Egypt
mohatef@zu.edu.eg, {hithamab,iziedan}@yahoo.com
[2]The British University; Dubai, UAE
Khaled.Shaalan@buid.ac.ae

Abstract. Named Entity Recognition (NER) task is an essential preprocessing task for many Natural Language Processing (NLP) applications such as text summarization, document categorization, Information Retrieval, among others. NER systems follow either rule-based approach or machine learning approach. In this paper, we introduce a novel NER system for Arabic using a hybrid approach, which combines a rule-based approach and a machine learning approach in order to improve the performance of Arabic NER. The system is able to recognize three types of named entities, including Person, Location and Organization. Experimental results on ANERcorp dataset showed that our hybrid approach has achieved better performance than using the rule-based approach and the machine learning approach when they are processed separately. It also outperforms the state-of-the-art hybrid Arabic NER systems.

1 Introduction

Named entity recognition (NER) is still an important task for improving the quality of many NLP applications such as Information Retrieval, Machine Translation, and Question Answering [1]. NER seeks to identify the sequence of words in a document that can be classified under a predefined category of named entity such as Person, Organization, and Location names. Arabic is a highly inflected language, with a rich morphology and complex syntax [2]. Generally, the significance of Arabic worldwide is too obvious to enumerate. The language is spoken by Arab world, and Islamic countries and communities. In this paper we concentrate on NER for Arabic. We integrate a rule-based NER component, a reproduction of NERA [3], with a machine learning NER component, in particular SVM, in order to obtain the advantages of both approaches and decrease their problems. The rule-based component depends on a set of grammar rules. Whereas, the machine learning component depends on a set of features extracted from the annotated text. The extracted features include morphological features that have been determined by the Morphological Analysis and Disambiguation for Arabic (MADA) tool[1][4] and gazetteer features (list of predefined NEs).

---

[1] http://www1.ccls.columbia.edu/MADA/

X. Shi and Y. Chen (Eds.): CWMT 2014, CCIS 493, pp. 93–103, 2014.
© Springer-Verlag Berlin Heidelberg 2014

We successfully could identify some recognition errors by simple grammar rules from the comparison between the results of the rule-based component and the results of the machine learning component.

The remainder of this paper is organized as follows. Section 2 introduces a background on NER. Section 3 describes the structure of our proposed hybrid system and its components. Experimental results are discussed in Section 4. In Section 5 we give some concluding remarks.

2   Background

Named Entity Recognition (NER) was first introduced in 1995 by the Message Understanding Conference (MUC-6)[2]. The named entity task is mainly defined as three subtasks: ENAMEX (for the Person, Location, and Organization), TIMEX (for Date and Time expressions), and NUMEX (for monetary amounts and percentages).

We focus on Arabic NER that has several challenges and characteristics:

- Lack of capital letters in the Arabic orthography: A named entity in Latin languages is usually distinguished by a capital letter at the word beginning. However, this is not the case in Arabic which makes the detection of NE in text based on the case of letters more difficult. Some efforts to overcome this problem have used lexical triggers that are derived from analyzing the NE's surrounding context [5] while some others have used the gloss feature of the English translation of the NE produced by the MADA tool [6].
- Complex Morphology: Arabic morphology is very complex because of the language agglutinative nature [7]. There are three types of agglutinative morphemes: stems, affixes and clitics. The primitive form of the word is the stem. Affix letters are attached to the stem which has three types: prefixes attached before the stem, suffixes attached after the stem, and circumfixes that surround the stem. Clitics are also attached to the stem after affixes. They play a syntactic role at the phase level. Clitics are either proclitics that precede the word or enclitics that follow the word. The conjunction "و" (wa[3], and) [8] and object pronoun "هن" (hn, they-3rdP-fem) are examples of proclitics and enclitics, respectively. A more general example is the word "وسيكتبونها" (wasayaktubuwnahA, and-they-will-write-it).
- Ambiguity: It is optional in modern Arabic texts to include diacritics which most often lead to ambiguous situations i.e. different meaning [9]. For example, consider the word علم Elm which if diacritized as عَلَمEalam it means the noun "flag" or if diacritized as عِلمEilm it means the noun "science". In addition to the optional diacritization problem, Arabic words can differ in meanings depending on the context in which it appears. Consider the following two sentences: قالت جريدة الشرق الأوسط إن الأسد باق في منصبه (qAlt jrydp Al$rq Al>wsT <n Al>sd bAq fy mnSbh, 'Asharq Al Awsat said that al-Assad will remain in his position') and الإرهاب قضية مهمة في منطقة

الشرق الأوسط (Al<rhAb qDyp mhmp fy mnTqp Al$rq Al>wsT, 'Terrorism is an important issue in the Middle East'). The named entity, الشرق الأوسط (Al$rq Al>wsT, Middle East) might represents either an Organization or a Location name which can be resolved from the context.

- Lack of Resources: The lack of Arabic NER freely available resources or the expense of creating or licensing these important Arabic NER resources make NER task far more challenging. So, researchers had to build their own resources. We used ANERcorp[4] Corpus that developed by [10] for both training and testing. The ANERcorp includes 4901 sentences with 150286 annotated words for the NER task. The total number of named entities is 12989 tokens.

The survey by Shaalan (2014) presents background and the progress made in Arabic NER research.

3   The Approach

Both machine learning-based and rule-based approaches have their own strengths and weaknesses and by combining them in one system they could achieve a better performance than applying each of them separately. To the best of our knowledge, the latest Arabic NER system has adopted the hybrid approach   was presented by Oudah and Shaalan [11]. The system   consists   of   two   dependent components   including rule-based   component   and   machine learning component where the output of rule-based   component   that represented as features   file is passed as an input to machine learning component . Thus, any classification error in rule-based component will be trained by the classifier which leads to an error in the whole system. In addition, any modification in the grammar rules or the gazetteers requires retraining the classification model again. Our novel hybrid approach aims to fix the previous problems with fully independent components. It consists of three main components: machine learning component, rule-based component, and tag selection and correction component.

3.1   The Machine Learning Component

Arabic NER is challenging due to the highly ambiguous nature of Arabic named entities (NEs). A NE can very well appear as a non-NE in Arabic text. Moreover, the modern style of Arabic writings allows for optional diacritization and different methods for performing transliterations. So, these peculiarities of the language raise the need for Machine Learning (ML) algorithms which lend itself to the Arabic NER task. These algorithms usually involve a selected set of features, extracted from datasets annotated with NEs, which is used to generate a statistical model for NE prediction. In the literature, the ML approaches used in NER systems are Maximum Entropy (ME) [12], Hidden Markov Model (HMM) [13], Conditional Random Fields (CRFs) [14], [15] and Support Vector Machines (SVM) [16].

---

[4] http://www1.ccls.columbia.edu/~ybenajiba/

The machine learning component uses SVM because of its robustness to noise and ability to deal with a large number of features effectively [17]. SVM is a supervised machine learning algorithm which is based on Neural Networks [16]. SVM learns to find a linear hyperplane which divides the elements (features) in space into positive and negative classes with maximal margin. We used YamCha toolkit[5] that converts the NER task to a text chunking task.

In Machine Learning-based NER approaches, there are two phases: training phase and test phase, as illustrated in Fig. 1. The first phase generates the classifier (model) by using a set of classification features. In the second phase, the classifier generated by the training phase is utilized to predict a class for each token (word).

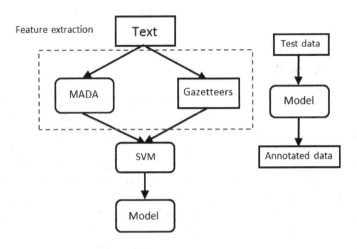

Fig. 1. Training and test phases

In the training phase each word is represented by a set of features and its actual NE's type in order to produce an SVM model that predicts the NE type. The selection of the subset to be utilized by a classifier is a very critical to the NER system's performance such that when optimized it can enhance the quality of the system dramatically. So, the first step in our hybrid approach is to extract the significant features from the training dataset. Then, we study the impact of each feature individually by adopting only one feature at a time and measure the system's performance in terms of F-measure metric. Finally, according to the performance achieved, we determine the optimized feature set for the proposed hybrid Arabic NER system.

3.2   The Feature Space

Feature selection refers to the task of identifying a useful subset of features chosen to represent elements of a larger set (i.e., the feature space). In the rest of this section, we discuss the feature space.

---

[5] http://chasen.org/·taku/software/yamcha/

- The word: It refers to the distribution of each NE type in the ANERcorp dataset. As shown in Table 1, the highest frequency is the Location NE. So, for example, the classifier would mostly recognize the sequence which consists of the word (الشرق, Al$rq) that is followed by the word الأوسط (Al>wsT, Middle) as a Location (East) name rather than an Organization (newspaper).

Table 1. Number of times each type was assigned to the word "الشرق" in ANERcorp

NE Type	Frequency
O	17
Person	0
Location	51
Organization	14
Total	82

- Contextual word feature (CXT): The features of a sliding window comprising a word n-gram that includes the candidate word, along with preceding and succeeding words For example, in the training corpus the verb "حضر" (HDr, attend) appears frequently before an NE of type Person. As such, the classifier will use this information to predict a Person NE after this verb.

- Gazetteer features (GAZ): A binary feature indicating the existence of the word in an individual gazetteer. In our hybrid system there are three gazetteers:
  — Location Gazetteer: countries, cities, rivers and mountains, etc.
  — Person Gazetteer: names of people.
  — Organizations Gazetteer: companies and other organizations.

- Morphological features (MORPH): A set of morphological information determined by MADA. We cover the following morphological features:
  — Aspect: One of the three aspects of the Arabic verb: perfective (ماضي, mADy), imperfective (مضارع, mDArE), or imperative (أمر, >mr).
  — Case: One of three cases of Arabic nominals: nominative (مرفوع, mrfwE), accusative (منصوب, mnSwb), or genitive (مجرور, mjrwr).
  — Gender: A binary value indicating the gender of the word, i.e. masculine or feminine.
  — Number: Any of the three values indicating the number of the word, i.e. singular, dual, or plural.
  — Mood: Any of the three Arabic moods that only vary for the imperfective verb: indicative (مرفوع, mrfwE), subjunctive (منصوب, mnSwb), or jussive (مجزوم, mjzwm).
  — State: Any of the three values: definite, indefinite, or construct.
  — Voice: A binary value indicating either passive or active voice.
  — Proclitics and Enclitics: exact clitics that are attached to the stem.

- Part-of-Speech (POS): A binary value indicating whether or not the POS tag (extracted by MADA) is a noun or proper noun.
- Gloss: A binary value indicating whether the English translation (gloss) provided by MADA starts with a capital letter.
- Lexical features (LEX): This feature considers the orthography of each token in the text. The usefulness of lexical features mostly appears when the same NE occurs in different places of the text but with some difference in the orthography. For example, in the sentence: أوباما يدافع عن برامج مراقبة الهواتف والإنترنت (>wbAmA ydAfE En brAmj mrAqbp AlhwAtf wAl<ntrnt, Obama defends program of surveillance phones and the Internet). Transliteration variant of foreign names is a common problem in Arabic writing. For example, Obama may be transliterated to Arabic as (أوباما, >wbAmA) or (أباما, >bAmA). So, in the training corpus, if Obama has only appeared with the first transliteration, the classifier cannot classify the second transliteration. However, when we used the last characters of the word as a feature, it would help the classifier to classify second transliteration also.

3.3 The Rule-Based Component

The initial version of the rule-based component is developed using the design documents of NERA, a NER system for Arabic [5] that is implemented using GATE[6]. Fig. 2 shows the construction of the Rule-based component. The system applies two procedures: firstly, recognizing and classifying NEs in text by the exact matching with gazetteers entries in the corresponding Person, Location and Organization Gazetteers. A sample of these gazetteers is shown in Table 2.

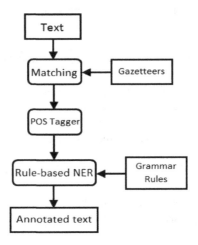

Fig. 2. Rule-based component

---

[6] http://gate.ac.uk/

Table 2. Sample entries in the three gazetteers

Complete Names	حسني مبارك
	Hsny mbArk
	Hosni Mubarak
City Names	الاسكندرية
	AlAskndryp
	Alexandria
Parties Names	الحزب الوطني الديمقراطي
	AlHzb AlwTny AldymqrATy
	National Democratic Party

Secondly, execute a finite-state transducer, based on a set of local grammar rules that are implemented using JAPE. The following example illustrates an implemented rule for recognizing an organization name. This rule identifies an organization name (token) that is preceded by a verb indicating an organization name (e.g."فاز", win) and followed by a nationality (e.g." الأردنية"", Jordanian).

```
Rule: ORG1
Priority:30
(
{Lookup.majorType=="verb-org"}
({Token}):Org1
({DAL})
)
-->
:Org1.Organization = {rule="ORG1"}
```

Fig. 3. A rule implemented in JAPE for recognizing organization name using surrounding indicators

JAPE rules depend also on Stanford POS Tagger[7] that assigns part of speech category to each word in the text. Often proper noun tags mark the existence of NEs in the text. So, based on this available information, we modified the preceding rule to verify whether or not the targeted token is a proper noun.

---

[7] http://nlp.stanford.edu/software/tagger.shtml

```
Rule: ORG1_modified
Priority:30
(
{Lookup.majorType=="verb-org"}
({Token,Token.category ==
noun_prop}):Org1
({DAL})
)
-->
:Org1.Organization = {rule="ORG1"}
```

Fig. 4. A rule implemented in JAPE for recognizing organization name using its POS category

3.4   Tag Selection and Correction Component

Fig. 5 shows the architecture of our proposed Arabic hybrid NER system.   The input data is applied in parallel to the rule-based and machine learning-based Arabic NER components. The tagging results for each component are compared with each other in order to agree on the final tags. The role of this component is to fine-tune the machine learning system's output by checking the most false negatives (i.e., missing annotations) and applying the correction using the tagging decisions determined by the rule-based component.

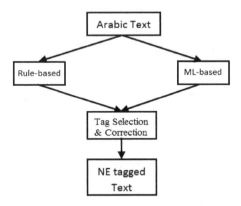

Fig. 5. Architecture of the hybrid System

4   Experiments and Results

In order to study the impact of the NER approaches we have examined each component separately before combining the results. In other words, we are dealing with three annotated outputs from the machine learning component, rule-based component, and the overall hybrid output, respectively. The experimental setting for the machine learning component uses splits of the ANERcorp dataset into three datasets: 90% as a training dataset, 5% as a development dataset, and 5% as a test dataset.

As far as the machine learning component is concerned, the experiment proceeds in three stages. In the first stage, the training is applied on the training dataset using selected feature set and the results are analyzed to determine the best feature set. In the second stage, the training is applied on the combined training and development datasets using the best selected feature set. In the third stage, the classifier is applied on the test dataset and the results are reported and discussed.

The baseline feature set consists of tokens at window size that ranges from -1/+1 to -4/+4.We found that a context size of one previous token and one subsequent token (i.e. window size is 3) achieves the best performance in this task. The baseline model has achieved a precision of 91.86% and recall of 48.78%. This indicates that adding extra features would improve the performance by increasing its coverage.

As far as the rule-based component is concerned, the untagged version of the reference dataset (i.e. ANERcorp) is entered to GATE for processing, where the annotated result can be automatically evaluated using Annotation Diff tool of GATE which has an elegant GUI for presenting the results. Three results were obtained from machine learning, rule-based and hybrid approaches in terms of the standard evaluation metric, i.e. Precision, Recall and F-measures [18], for Person, Organization and Location, as presented in Table 3. This table shows that the results from machine learning approach (SVM) are better than that from rule-based approach whereas the hybrid system performs the best. Table 4 shows that our hybrid system outperforms the state-of-the-art Arabic hybrid NER system by [11].

Table 3. performance of each component in the system

Approach	Type	P	R	F
Machine Learning	PER	97.67	93.33	95.45
	ORG	89.19	88.00	88.59
	LOC	96.12	88.84	92.34
Rule-based	PER	97.98	90.00	93.82
	ORG	81.29	92.67	86.60
	LOC	95.26	88.05	91.51
Hybrid	PER	97.01	96.30	96.65
	ORG	90.00	96.00	92.90
	LOC	95.18	94.42	94.80

Table 4. Comparing best results of (Oudahand Shaalan, 2012) with our best results

	PER	ORG	LOC
Oudah and Shaalan, 2012	94.4	88. 2	90.1
Our approach	96.65	92.9	94.8

5   Conclusions

Our proposed hybrid NER approach integrates the rule-based approach with the ML-based approach in order to optimize overall performance. The two components responsible for the integrated approached are processed in parallel. A tag selection and correction component is used in order to fine-tune the machine learning system's output by checking the most false negatives (i.e., missing annotations) and applying the correction using the tagging decisions determined by the rule-based component. Experimental results on ANERcorp dataset, with F-measure have shown 96.65%, 92.9%, and 94.8% for Person, Organization, and Location, respectively. Therefore, our hybrid system outperforms the state-of-the-art of the Arabic hybrid NER system. Our study on the impact of the features indicates that when window size is 3 it achieves the best performance. For future work, the authors would like to increase the capability of the system in identifying other types of named entities. We are also considering the possibility of investigating different machine learning techniques other than SVM and study their impact on the overall performance of the hybrid NER system.

References

1. Benajiba, Y., Diab, M., Rosso, P.: Arabic Named Entity Recognition using Optimized Feature Sets. In: Proceedings of the 2008 Conference on Empirical Methods in Natural Language Processing, Honolulu, pp. 284–293 (2008)
2. Al-Sughaiyer, I.A., Al-Kharashi, I.A.: Arabic morphological analysis techniques: a comprehensive survey. Journal of the American Society for Information Science and Technology 55(2004), 189–213 (2004)
3. Shaalan, K., Raza, H.: NERA: Named entity recognition for arabic. Journal of the American Society for Information Science and Technology, 1652–1663 (2009)
4. Habash, N., Rambow, O., Roth, R.: MADA+TOKAN: A Toolkit for Arabic Tokenization, Diacritization, Morphological Disambiguation, POS Tagging, Stemming and Lemmatization. In: Proceedings of MEDAR, Cairo, Egypt, pp. 102–109 (2009)
5. Shaalan, K., Raza, H.: Arabic Named Entity Recognition from Diverse Text Types. In: Nordström, B., Ranta, A. (eds.) GoTAL 2008. LNCS (LNAI), vol. 5221, pp. 440–451. Springer, Heidelberg (2008)
6. Farber, B., Freitag, D., Habash, N., Rambow, O.: Improving NER in Arabic Using a Morphological Tagger. In: Proceedings of LREC 2008 (2008)
7. Habash, N.Y.: Introduction to Arabic Natural Language Processing. Mogran & Claypool Publisher (2010)
8. Habash, N., Soudi, A., Buckwalter, T.: On Arabic transliteration. In: Arabic Computational Morphology: Knowledge-based and Empirical Methods. Kluwer/Springer (2007)

9. Shaalan, K.: A Survey of Arabic Named Entity Recognition and Classification. Computational Linguistics 40(2), 469–510 (2014)
10. Benajiba, Y., Rosso, P., BenedíRuiz, J.M.: ANERsys: An Arabic Named Entity Recognition System Based on Maximum Entropy. In: Gelbukh, A. (ed.) CICLing 2007. LNCS, vol. 4394, pp. 143–153. Springer, Heidelberg (2007)
11. Oudah, M., Shaalan, K.: A pipeline Arabic named entity recognition using a hybrid approach. In: Proceedings of the 24th International Conference on Computational Linguistics, COLING 2012, India, pp. 2159–2176 (2012)
12. Borthwick, A.: A Maximum Entropy Approach to Named Entity Recognition Ph.D. thesis, Computer Science Department, New York University (1999)
13. Bikel, D.M., Schwartz, R.L., Weischedel, R.M.: An Algorithm that Learns What's in a Name. Machine Learning 34(1-3), 211–231 (1999)
14. Lafferty, J.D., McCallum, A., Pereira, F.C.N.: Conditional random fields: Probabilistic models for segmenting and labeling sequence data. In: Proceedings of the Eighteenth International Conference on Machine Learning, pp. 282–289 (2001)
15. McCallum, A., Li, W.: Early Results for Named Entity Recognition with Conditional Random Fields, Feature Induction and Web-Enhanced Lexicons. In: Proceedings of Seventh Conference on Natural Language Learning, CoNLL 2003 (2003)
16. Vapnik, V.: The Nature of Statistical Learning Theory. Springer, Heidelberg (1995)
17. Benajiba, Y., Diab, M., Rosso, P.: Arabic named entity recognition: An svm-based approach. In: The International Arab Conference on Information Technology, ACIT 2008 (2008)
18. Sitter, A.D., Calders, T., Daelemans, W.: A Formal Framework for Evaluation of Information Extraction, University of Antwerp, Dept. of Mathematics and Computer Science, Technical Report, TR 2004-0 (2004)

Reexaminatin on Voting
for Crowd Sourcing MT Evaluation

Yiming Wang[1,*] and Muyun Yang[2]

[1]Harbin Institute of Technology, Harbin, China
wangvince2110@163.com
[2]Harbin Institute of Technology, Harbin, China
ymy@mtlab.hit.edu.cn

Abstract. We describe a model based on Ranking Support Vector Machine(SVM) used to deal with the crowdsourcing data. Our model focuses on how to use poor quality crowdsourcing data to get high quality sorted data. The data sets, used for model training and testing, has the situation of data missing. And we found that our model achieves better results than voting model in all the cases in our experiment, including sorting of two translations and four translations.

Keywords: crowdsourcing, automatic evaluation of machine translation, voting model, SVM model, data missing.

1   Introduction

In natural language processing, artificial intelligence, information retrieval, etc., human evaluations are the first standard, making it crucial to obtain human evaluation data for these studies. For a long time, these data rely on a small group of expert evaluation and the price are very high. Also, because of the subjective differences, we usually need many annotators to make evaluation on the same data during data collection, and this raises the cost of data collection. However, crowdsourcing gives researchers a new choice in these fields.

Crowdsourcing is coined by Jeff Howe and Mark Robinson in 2006 [1], defined as representing the act of a company or institution taking a function once performed by employees and outsourcing it to an undefined (and generally large) network of people in the form of an open call. This can take the form of peer-production (when the job is performed collaboratively), but is also often undertaken by sole individuals. The crucial prerequisite is the use of the open call format and the large network of potential laborers.

Although the concept of crowdsourcing was only made in 2006, its applications are earlier than there, and the most famous one is reCAPTCHA project. This project is being applied to more than 40,000 websites, and has helped solve about 400 million words of texts from scanned documents. A normal crowdsourcing platform should include a publish part of task, a work part for annotators and a payment part. Amazon

---

* Corresponding author.

X. Shi and Y. Chen (Eds.): CWMT 2014, CCIS 493, pp. 104–115, 2014.
© Springer-Verlag Berlin Heidelberg 2014

Mechanical Turk is one of the most famous crowdsourcing platforms. Researchers can get a lot of cheap human evaluation in a short time through this platform. Although data from a single annotator can have high disagreement with expert data, with the increasing of annotators and quality control methods, these data can reach to almost the same quality with expert data [2, 3]. Then, more and more researchers introduce crowdsourcing into their own studies. In picture tagging, information retrieval, corpus collection, data mining and other fields, crowdsourcing platforms have been widely used [4, 5, 6, 7, 8, 9, 10].

The most critical issue of applications of crowdsourcing is how to get high quality data extracting from the data of poor quality. Because the results are used as standards answers of followed studies, post-processing of crowdsourcing data is more important for translation evaluation ranking than other fields.

In this paper, we focus on the sentence level translations rankings and address models for crowdsourcing data processing. Then we explore the impact of cases of missing data on the different models. Firstly, we analyze the data, collected from a crowdsourcing platform, and find the quality of the data is poor. Then, we chose two models: voting model and ranking SVM model. For each model, we have carried out experiments on different kinds of data missing and find that in either case, ranking SVM model has achieved better results than voting model.

2   Related Work

The early work of crowdsourcing data processing was mainly focused on the task of labeling. In the study of Jacob Whitehill, etc, they set tasks to different difficulty levels, and set annotators to different confidence levels. Then they made experiment with the EM algorithm [11]. Vikas C.Raykar et al tried using a logistic regression classifier instead of EM algorithm in 2010 [12]. Yan Yan et al extended the study of confidence, they set different confidence levels with different tasks [13]. When it was in 2011, Vikas C.Raykar et al worked on double labeling tasks, multi-labeling tasks and ranking tasks to find out the way to set confidence of annotators, and they used EM algorithm to sort annotators, with the purpose of separating malicious annotators [14]. These studies just gave some methods to translate ranking tasks into labeling tasks. But ranking tasks and labeling tasks are quite different while the ranking data contains logic. For A > B, B > C, C > B, a very likely outcome is accepting these data and come to the result with a "ring" using approach of labeling tasks. And for the ranking task, it has to give up one of the data to get the results without a "ring".

During working on ranking tasks of crowdsourcing, researchers got similar conclusions with snow. These studies found the quality of a single annotator is poor, but the data of a number of annotators can even exceed expert data with voting model. Early works also showed that adding confidence estimation to annotators can improve the results [15]. In WMT2013, this method had been used into practice [16]. Recently there has been a new model for ranking tasks——Bradley-Terry model. This model can retain more logical information contained in the original data compared with voting model, but it can't work directly on original data, so researchers build a pretreatment to estimating confidence of annotators [17].

Compared with these studies, our work mainly has two differences. First, these studies treat annotators and data with two different models, while our model processes these two parts together and directly output the result of ranking. Second, a common case of crowdsourcing data is data missing. Although some of these studies had mentioned this case, the impact of data missing on models didn't been analyzed. We divide the case of data missing into two categories:

1. Annotators missing. This case means that some annotators   doesn't finish all tasks
2. Logic missing. This case means that there are some logic missing on tasks. For example, there are translations A, B and C. In order to obtain ranking data on the crowdsourcing platform, we usually ask annotators to evaluate pairs (A, B), (A, C) and (B, C). However, due to positiveness of different annotators, we can only get data of pairs (A, B) and (A, C) sometimes and miss the data of pair (B, C).

We explore the impact of these cases on voting model and ranking SVM model.

3   Models for Crowd Sourcing MT Evaluation on Ranking

We select three models for our experiment. The first is the most simple model——simple voting model. Although there are many improved models, voting model is still the most common model for crowdsourcing. There are three main reasons:

1. The accuracy of voting model is acceptable
2. Voting model is very simple and easy to improve to a variety of versions for different tasks
3. Improved methods are usually complicated and do not increase the accuracy obviously

A simple way to improve voting model is weighted voting model. This model analyze confidence of annotators before voting and this can enhance the accuracy significantly. Here, we chose this model as our second experimental model.

Ranking SVM model is our third experimental model. It's a kind of machine learning model which can directly working on original ranking data. The performance of ranking SVM usually depends on feature selecting.

3.1   Simple Voting Model

Simple voting model is the most basic form of voting. This model treats each evaluation of every annotator as one equal vote. When there is a winner of evaluation, the vote will vote to the winner and when all parts have equal quality, every part get votes. Here we use the following scoring:

$$vote_{k_{ij}} = \begin{cases} 2 & i > j \\ 1 & i = j, all\ good \\ -1 & i < j, all\ bad \\ -2 & i < j \end{cases} \quad (k\ is\ the\ annotator) \quad (1)$$

Let i is one of the translations, n is the number of annotators who have evaluated on translation i, and k is one of these annotators. When m_k is the count of pairs which annotator k evaluated translation i, the $score_i$ of translation i set as:

$$score_i = \frac{1}{\sum_{k=1}^{n} m_k} \sum_{k=1}^{n} \sum_{j=1}^{m_k} vote_{kij} \tag{2}$$

After finished these, we rank translations by the scores. This model allows some translations are equal.

This model is very simple and has a good robustness of noise. But this model has two shortages:

1. Simple voting model treats every annotator as equal, and this makes it week when there are malicious annotators.
2. Simple voting model gives up logical information which contains in original data, and this makes the model can't distinguish votes from different pairs.

3.2   Weighted Voting Model

Weighted voting model solves the first shortage of simple voting model coarsely. This model treats different annotators with different confidence levels.

Here, we divide parts of the data as training set and testing set. Then we get agreements between annotators and the expert on the training set as confidence vels. $vote_{kij}$ comes from formula (1), and the score of translation i is calculated by following formula:

$$score_i = \frac{1}{\sum_{k=1}^{n} m_k} \sum_{k=1}^{n} \sum_{j=1}^{m_k} (vote_{kij} \times weight_k) \tag{3}$$

Let $weight_k$ be the confidence level of annotator k, which is the agreement with the expert on training set.

This model solves the first shortage of simple voting model, but the solution is very rough. This weight distribution program agrees more with subjective judgments, but there is no strict scientific potential, Because of its simple and effective way, this model has been widely used.

The second shortage of simple voting model can't be solved by voting model. An alternative is not to vote directly on the translation, but pairs of translations. However, in practice, the number of annotators in each pair of translations usually is small, so that the alternative losses statistical significance and it is rarely used.

3.3   Ranking Support Vector Machine (SVM)

SVM model is a machine learning method, it based on the idea that when the classifier in the case that linear separable and the target is linear inseparable, we can project the target onto the high dimension by non-linear mapping until the target become separable. The non-linear mapping used in the method is called core function. Core function is the SVM model's essence, because usually when we promote the dimension, it will cause the computing increases in a geometric way, eventually leading to the curse of dimension disaster. But with the SVM core function expansion theorem, we do not need to explicitly know about the function form, so, when the dimension goes up, the calculation do not increase, thus avoiding the curse of dimensionality.

The earliest SVM model supports two models, classification and regression, with the theory developing, ranking SVM model is also presented. Using ranking SVM model, we can get a better sorting result than traditional SVM models, so the ranking SVM model gets used widely in cases that we do not need to know the target predicted value explicitly but only need to know target ranking.

The key point that impacts the result of SVM model is feature selection. Here, in order to preserve all the information in the original data, we design a basic feature, which sets a feature for R_{ij} of each translation. Meanwhile, i should be less than j, meaning R_{ji} does not exist. For every annotator, they all have their own basic features, meaning when there are n annotators and m basic features, the total number of the features is n*m. For annotator k, the feature values as follows and $vote_{k_{ij}}$ comes from formula (1):

$$feature_{k_{R_{ij}}} = \begin{cases} vote_{k_{ij}} & for\ translation\ i \\ -vote_{k_{ij}} & for\ translation\ j \end{cases} \tag{4}$$

This design of features can solve two shortages of simple voting model. We can separate different annotators and keep the logical information of the original data at the same time. Meanwhile, we consider the results of weighing voting model as a backup feature, then do experiments with voting results and non-voting results separately.

4   Our Experiment

4.1   Data Collection

We collected 300 Chinese sentences and translations of these sentences from four translation systems: baidu, bing, youdao and google. In these translations, there are 180 tasks having two different translations, and the four translations of the rest 120 tasks are all different. Meanwhile, we got the ranking of each group's translation which was used as the standard data.

We split translations from four systems into six pairwise translation pairs, every annotator only evaluated one of the six translation pairs. When evaluating the translations, annotators have four choices: A is better than B; A is worse than B; both are bad; both are good.

We counted the number of tasks annotators completed, and found that different annotators had a large difference in evaluating amount. The result is shown in Figure 1.

As can be seen from the figure, no matter there are four or two translations, most annotators completed 100 or less tasks, and many annotators only completed no more than 10 tasks. We think these annotators which completed less than 10 tasks have no statistical significance, so we don't accept these data, which means we have 17 anno-tators' data. But at the meantime, we noticed that, there are 6 annotators completed almost all tasks in two cases. In comparison, when there are two translations, the completed tasks' number of annotators are at average, but when there are four transla-tions, the number between annotators has a large difference.

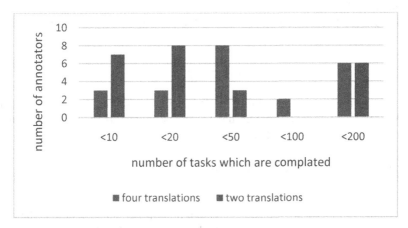

Fig. 1. Data of Annotators

4.2   Experiment on Two Translations

There are 180 tasks of two translations and as we all know, when the data only has two translations, the voting model implicitly contains the logical information of the evaluating data. After analyzing the data, we find that in the case where the data only has two translations, there are five annotators completing the same 76 tasks, so we consider these 76 tasks as the data without annotators missing, and consider all 180 tasks as the data with annotators missing. Because there are only two translations, we don't need to care about whether lacking of logic.

In each dataset, we try to divide the experiment data into ten parts equally. All an-notators of the experiment are included in each part of the data. We pick up one part of data and put it into training dataset every time, and use the rest parts as testing dataset. We have experiments on all four models including simple voting, weighted voting, ranking SVM with voting results and ranking SVM without voting results in all two cases of data missing, and the results are shown in figure 3.

4.3   Experiment on Four Translations

The experiment of four translations is quite same with that of two translations. There are 120 tasks of four translations, and there are six annotators completing all 120 tasks, meanwhile, their evaluating data miss one pair of translation's evaluation. Then we consider data of these six annotators as the data without annotators missing but logic missing, and consider data of all annotators as the data with annotators missing.

The method of data dividing and experiment is the same with that of two translations, and the results are shown in figure 4.

4.4   Analysis

Agreement of Annotators
Here, we use the Cohen's kappa [18] method to analyze agreements between annotators and the expert. The formula is defined as:

$$\kappa = \frac{P(O)-P(E)}{1-P(E)} \tag{5}$$

P (O) is defined as the probability of two annotators having the same evaluation, this probability can counted through data. P (E) is defined as the probability of two annotators having the same evaluation by chance.

$$P(E) = P(A > B)^2 + P(A = B, all\ good)^2 + P(A = B, all\ bad)^2 + P(A < B)^2 \tag{6}$$

In each item of P (E), we use square symbol to indicate that each item is the probability calculated of two annotators [16]. And each item of P (E) can be directly calculated through the collecting data.

Normally, when kappa value is within 0~0.2, means extremely low consistency, 0.21~0.40, means general consistency, 0.41~0.60, means moderate consistency, 0.61~0.80, means high consistency, 0.81~1.00, means almost exactly the same. We compared agreement between every annotator and expert data. The results are shown in Figure 2.

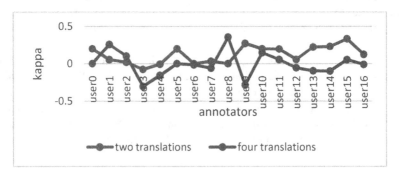

Fig. 2. Agreement of annotators and expert data

As can be seen from the figure, when there are two translations, parts of consistency of the annotators' data and the experts' data are within 0 to 0.3, which belong to extremely low consistency. When there are four translations, the consistency is hovering around 0, which is obviously lower than the case with two translations. This feature shows crowdsourcing data is a kind of data which is low consistency and poor quality

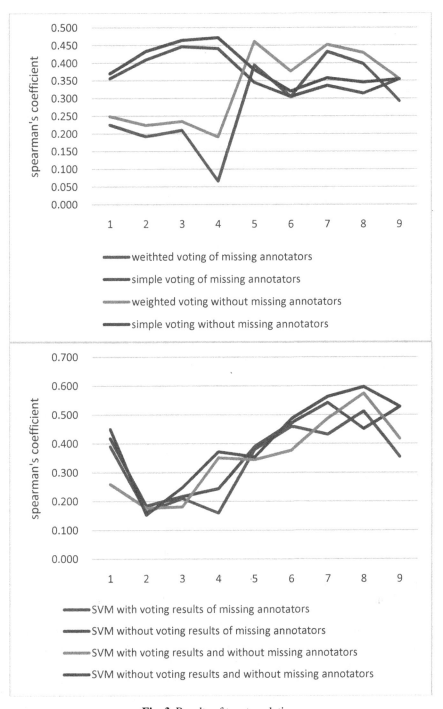

Fig. 3. Results of two translations

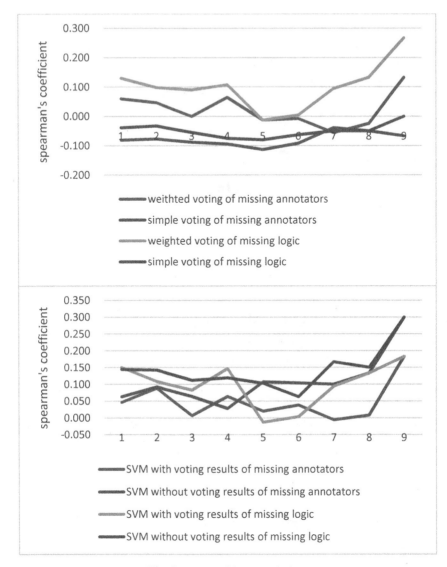

Fig. 4. Results of four translations

Finding of Two Translations

In figure 3, numbers of abscissa means the number of parts of data using as training dataset.

We can find out when the number of parts of training data is more than 5, results of weighted voting model are better than simple voting model. But the simple one is better than the weighted one when lack of training data.

Ranking SVM model is better than voting model in all cases and seems need less data for training to get the same results. It has a great influence on the SVM model when voting results are used as features of SVM model, and the SVM model shows strong synchronization. Ranking SVM model seems to be better without the voting model, but the effect depends on the raw data.

The results without annotators missing are better than that lacking in logic in all models. And this is less obvious in SVM model.

Finding of Four Translations
In figure 4, numbers of abscissa means the number of parts of data using as training dataset.

The similar result is achieved as the case of two translations. The difference is more obvious between weighted voting model and simple voting model. Weighted voting model is much better compared with simple voting.

The advantage of SVM model compared with voting model is also more obvious. The results of SVM model without voting are still better than that with voting. However the difference is less obvious.

We can clearly find that data missing has a serious impact on voting model, while missing annotators is more destructive. Instead of using all the annotators' data, using only annotators who completed all tasks can get better results. Although SVM model shows the same characteristic, it has a better robustness and can get amazing results on dataset with data missing.

5   Conclusion

First, we analyze of the collected data, and found there is a lack of consistency between annotators' data and expert data, which reflects that the quality of crowdsourcing data is quite low.

Then, we made the research under the condition of two translations and four translations respectively, tried a simple voting model, weighted voting model and ranking SVM model. We also tried to add results of the voting model to the SVM model.

During the experiment we divided the data into two cases: annotators missing and Logic missing, and make the experiment under different cases. Through the experiment we found that the simple voting model has a quality of good performance when there is little data for training, but the overall accuracy is not high. When join the weighted voting model and ranking SVM model, the results are better than the simple voting model. We also found that ranking SVM model usually needs less training data compared with weighted voting model.

When compared the ranking SVM model with voting model, the SVM model is always better than the results of the voting model, and when added with voting model, the result of the ranking SVM model becomes more relatively stable. The ranking SVM model seems to be better without the voting model, but the effect depends on the raw data.

For cases when lack of both of annotators and logical information, all models are more sensitive to the absence of annotators, instead of using all the annotators' data, using only annotators who completed all tasks can get better results. In comparison, the model of vote is more sensitive to the two kinds of evaluation lack, while the impact on the ranking SVM model increase and decrease as the task complexity varies. For logic missing, the ranking SVM model can deduce the results better, while voting model performance is much worse.

Acknowledgments. This work is supported by the NSF China (Grant No. 61272384, 61105072 & 61402134).

References

1. Howe, J.: Crowdsourcing: A definition. Crowdsourcing: Tracking the rise of the amateur (2006)
2. Snow, R., O'Connor, B., Jurafsky, D., Ng, A.Y.: Cheap and fast—but is it good?: evaluating non-expert annotations for natural language tasks. In: Proceedings of the Conference on Empirical Methods in Natural Language Processing, pp. 254–263. Association for Computational Linguistics (2008)
3. Kittur, A., Chi, E.H., Suh, B.: Crowd sourcing user studies with Mechanical Turk. In: Proceedings of the SIGCHI Conference on Human Factors in Computing Systems, pp. 453–456. ACM (2008)
4. Sorokin, A., Forsyth, D.: Utility data annotation with amazon mechanical turk. Urbana 51, 820 (2008)
5. Novotney, S., Callison-Burch, C.: Cheap, fast and good enough: Automatic speech recogni- tion with non-expert transcription. In: Human Language Technologies: The 2010 Annual Conference of the North American Chapter of the Association for Computational Linguistics, pp. 207–215. Association for Computational Linguistics (2010)
6. Kazai, G., Kamps, J., Koolen, M., Milic-Frayling, N.: Crowdsourcing for book search evaluation: impact of hit design on comparative system ranking. In: Proceedings of the 34th International ACM SIGIR Conference on Research and Development in Information Retrieval, pp. 205–214. ACM (2011)
7. Xintong, G., Hongzhi, W., Song, Y., Hong, G.: Brief survey of crowdsourcing for data mining. Expert Systems with Applications 41, 7987–7994 (2014)
8. Fort, K., Adda, G., Sagot, B., Mariani, J., Couillault, A.: Crowdsourcing for Language Resource Development: Criticisms About Amazon Mechanical Turk Overpowering Use. In: Vetulani, Z., Mariani, J. (eds.) LTC 2011. LNCS, vol. 8387, pp. 303–314. Springer, Heidelberg (2014)
9. Callison-Burch, C., Dredze, M.: Creating speech and language data with Amazon's Mechanical Turk. In: Proceedings of the NAACL HLT 2010 Workshop on Creating Speech and Lan- guage Data with Amazon's Mechanical Turk, pp. 1–12. Association for Computational Linguistics (2010)
10. Lawson, N., Eustice, K., Perkowitz, M., Yetisgen-Yildiz, M.: Annotating large email datasets for named entity recognition with Mechanical Turk. In: Proceedings of the NAACL HLT 2010 Workshop on Creating Speech and Language Data with Amazon's Mechanical Turk, pp. 71–79. Association for Computational Linguistics (2010)
11. Whitehill, J., Wu, T., Bergsma, J., Movellan, J.R., Ruvolo, P.L.: Whose vote should count more: Optimal integration of labels from labelers of unknown expertise. In: Advances in Neural Information Processing Systems, pp. 2035–2043 (2009)
12. Raykar, V.C., Yu, S., Zhao, L.H., Valadez, G.H., Florin, C., Bogoni, L., Moy, L.: Learning from crowds. The Journal of Machine Learning Research 11, 1297–1322 (2010)

13. Yan, Y., Rosales, R., Fung, G., Schmidt, M.W., Valadez, G.H., Bogoni, L., Moy, L., Dy, J.G.: Modeling annotator expertise: Learning when everybody knows a bit of something. In: International Conference on Artificial Intelligence and Statistics, pp. 932–939 (2010)
14. Raykar, V.C., Yu, S.: Ranking annotators for crowdsourced labeling tasks. In: Advances in Neural Information Processing Systems, pp. 1809–1817 (2011)
15. Callison-Burch, C.: Fast, cheap, and creative: evaluating translation quality using Amazon's Mechanical Turk. In: Proceedings of the 2009 Conference on Empirical Methods in Natural Language Processing, vol. 1, pp. 286–295. Association for Computational Linguistics (2009)
16. Bojar, O., Buck, C., Callison-Burch, C., Federmann, C., Haddow, B., Koehn, P., Monz, C., Post, M., Soricut, R., Specia, L.: Findings of the 2013 workshop on statistical machine trans- lation. In: Proceedings of the Eighth Workshop on Statistical Machine Translation, pp. 1–44 (2013)
17. Chen, X., Bennett, P.N., Collins-Thompson, K., Horvitz, E.: Pairwise ranking aggregation in a crowdsourced setting. In: Proceedings of the Sixth ACM International Conference on Web Search and Data Mining, pp. 193–202. ACM (2013)
18. Landis, J.R., Koch, G.G.: The measurement of observer agreement for categorical data. Biometrics, 159–174 (1977)

Author Index

Bakr, Hitham M. Abo   93

Chao, Lidia S.   13, 24
Chen, Lei   49

Dong, Rui   61

Hao, Jie   1

Jin, Yaohong   33

Leal, Ana   70
Li, Miao   49
Li, Xiao   61
Liu, Xiaodie   33
Liu, Yang   1
Lu, Chunhui   70
Lu, Yi   13

Ma, Bo   61
Meselhi, Mohamed A.   93
Mi, Chenggang   61

Quaresma, Paulo   70

Schmaltz, Márcia   70
Shaalan, Khaled   93

Wang, Lei   61
Wang, Longyue   13, 24
Wang, Yiming   24
Wang, Yiming   104
Wong, Derek F.   13, 24
Wu, Peihao   80

Xie, Jun   80
Xu, Jinan   80

Yang, Muyun   104
Yang, Yating   61
Yang, Zhenxin   49

Zhang, Dakun   1
Zhang, Jiajun   1
Zhang, Jian   49
Zhang, Yujie   80
Zhu, Yun   33
Zhu, Zede   49
Ziedan, Ibrahim   93